Herbert Puchta & Jeff Stranks

with Richard Carter & Peter Lewis-Jones

English in Mind

Second edition

Workbook 3

CAMBRIDGE
UNIVERSITY PRESS

Welcome section

1 Present simple vs. present continuous

Complete the sentences. Use the present simple or present continuous form of the verbs.

I'm Christy Bell, and I'm in Year 11 at a school in Manchester. This is my big GCSE exam year, so I [1] _don't have_ (not have) as much free time as I did before. When I [2] _____ (not do) my homework or studying for tests, I try to see my friends. Saturday night is really the only time when everyone's free, because most of my friends [3] _____ (work) on Saturdays. I have a job in a home and garden centre, but now it [4] _____ (get) harder to find enough time to do that and all of my school work too. I [5] _____ (need) the money, though, because I don't get any pocket money from my mum. I [6] _____ (do) some babysitting, which is good because I usually [7] _____ (get) my school work done at the same time, and I get paid for it!

Most of the boys in my class seem to spend a lot of their free time on computers. More and more of them [8] _____ (get) computer games, or doing online gaming, but I don't like them much. And these days people [9] _____ (use) instant messaging to talk to friends, but I [10] _____ (prefer) texting my friends on my mobile – I hate sitting in front of a computer for hours. I do enough of that with my homework!!

2 Question tags

Complete each question tag. Write one word in each space.

1 He's just a child, _____ _isn't_ _____ he?

2 It isn't easy being a teenager, _____ it?

3 They're only 3 and 4 years old – they're just toddlers, _____ they?

4 Leaving a tap on wastes water, _____ it?

5 You recycled that paper, _____ you?

6 We can't go on destroying the rainforests, _____ we?

7 Your sister's just had a baby, _____ she?

8 We shouldn't drop litter on the streets, _____ we?

9 The atmosphere's become very polluted, _____ it?

10 One day you'll be a pensioner, _____ you?

3 Describing someone's age and the environment

Find twelve words in the wordsnake. Write them in the correct columns.

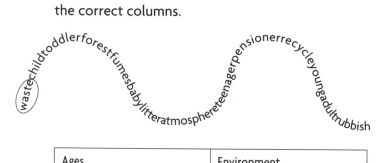

wastechildtoddlerforestfumesbabylitteratmosphereteenagerpensionerrecycleyoungadultrubbish

Ages	Environment
	waste

B

1 Ways of talking about the future

a Read the sentences. Mark them *A* if it is an arrangement, *P* if it is a prediction or *I* if it is an intention.

1 'I've decided on a subject to study at university – Biology.' `I`

2 'We've arranged to visit my grandparents on Saturday.' ☐

3 'My dad? Give me money to buy a new computer? Definitely not!' ☐

4 'I phoned the doctor and made an appointment to see her tomorrow morning.' ☐

5 'Planes fly from London to Australia in ten hours in the future? Yes, definitely.' ☐

6 'My friend Mike has decided to leave school next year.' ☐

b Use the underlined words in Exercise 1b to make sentences: for arrangement use present continuous; for prediction use *will/won't*; for intention use *going to*.

1 *I'm going to study Biology at university.*

2 ....

3 ....

4 ....

5 ....

6 ....

2 Musical instruments

Match the words with the pictures. Write a–f in the boxes.

1 keyboards `e`   4 piano ☐
2 trumpet ☐   5 flute ☐
3 drums ☐   6 guitar ☐

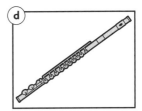
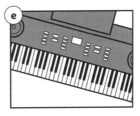

3 Medicine and health

Circle the correct words.

1 He fell over in town and broke his leg. An *ambulance* / *injection* took him to hospital.

2 I went to the doctor and she gave me *a surgeon* / *an injection*.

3 If you carry that heavy bag, you might *hurt* / *pain* yourself.

4 I hit my leg this morning, and now it's really *hurt* / *sore*.

5 Thousands of people are ill – it's a big *epidemic* / *cold*.

6 She's got a headache and a very high *temperature* / *pain*.

7 My uncle had to see the doctor because of the *sore* / *pain* in his back.

8 Some doctors in Britain complain that they've got too many *injections* / *patients*.

C

1 Present perfect simple with *for* or *since*

a Complete the sentences with *for* or *since*.

1 Pietro has been in England ____since____ the start of the summer.

2 He has studied English _____ he was seven years old.

3 His mother has been with him in England _____ two weeks.

4 He hasn't eaten any fish and chips _____ he arrived.

5 He hasn't had a good cup of coffee _____ he left Italy.

6 He hasn't seen his friends _____ a long time.

b Make sentences with the present perfect of the underlined verb and *for* or *since*.

1 I <u>have</u> a bicycle. My parents gave it to me last year. *I've had my bicycle for a year / since last year.*

2 I'<u>m</u> in this class. I joined the class six months ago. _____

3 Joanna and I <u>are</u> friends. We became friends in 2009. _____

4 I <u>know</u> Paul Carpenter. I first met him a year ago. _____

2 British vs. American English

Sally is a British teenager. She's writing to her new American friend, Mina. Find eight words (one on each line) that Mina might not understand. Change them into American English.

Hi Mina

My name's Sally and I'm going to tell you about myself. I live in London. Our ~~flat~~   *apartment*

is on the tenth floor so we have to go up in a lift to get to it! The place where we live is OK   _____

but unfortunately a lot of people around here throw rubbish on the street instead of putting   _____

it in the bin, so the pavements get dirty and that's not really very nice, is it? Anyway, what   _____

else can I tell you? Well, I like sport a lot, especially football, but I don't play it, I just watch   _____

it on TV. I think perhaps I should do some sport because I eat a lot! I just love biscuits and   _____

most days I eat a lot of sweets too, so I'm not the healthiest person in the world! Starting   _____

next week, though, I'm going to start cycling to school (now I use the underground), so that   _____

will help me to get fit, I hope!

Write soon and tell me about yourself, OK?! Bye!

3 Homes

Match the words and their definitions. Write a–f in the boxes.

1 detached	[c]	a a machine that takes you from one floor to another
2 garage	[ ]	b a 'house' on wheels
3 garden	[ ]	c not connected to other houses
4 flat	[ ]	d a place to keep cars
5 lift	[ ]	e an area near a house with grass and flowers
6 caravan	[ ]	f a home on one floor of a large building

D

1 used to [do]

Look at the information about people who have changed things in their lives. Write sentences.

name	in the past	now		
Paul	meat	fish	(eat)	1 *Paul used to eat meat, but now he eats fish.*
Sandra	tea	coffee	(drink)	2 ....
Amanda	dog	cat	(have)	3 ....
June	magazines	newspapers	(read)	4 ....
Gregory	car	bicycle	(drive/ride)	5 ....
Daniel	TV	sport	(watch/play)	6 ....

2 mustn't vs. don't have to

Circle the correct words.

1 You *don't have to* / *mustn't* drive fast – we've got lots of time.

2 You *don't have to* / *mustn't* drive fast – this road is full of holes and very dangerous.

3 You *don't have to* / *mustn't* buy a new laptop – they're much too expensive.

4 You *don't have to* / *mustn't* buy a new laptop – I can fix your old one easily.

5 You *don't have to* / *mustn't* tell Sarah about the party – I invited her last night.

6 You *don't have to* / *mustn't* tell James about the party – I really don't want him to know about it!

7 You *don't have to* / *mustn't* get up today – it's a holiday!

8 You *don't have to* / *mustn't* get up today – the doctor told me to stay in bed.

9 You *don't have to* / *mustn't* wash my new shirt – it can only be dry-cleaned.

10 You *don't have to* / *mustn't* wash my new shirt – it isn't dirty.

3 Information technology

Complete the crossword puzzle.

1 With a laptop, you can use a mouse or a touch ____pad____ .

2 Find the programme on the internet and then _____ it – it's free!

3 I couldn't type anything – the _____ was broken!

4 To access this site, you need to log _____ first.

5 I had to buy a new power _____ for my laptop.

6 Put the CD into the _____ and it will run automatically.

7 My dad just installed a new wi-fi _____ at home.

8 How many USB _____ has this computer got?

9 I remember my username – but I can't remember the _____ !

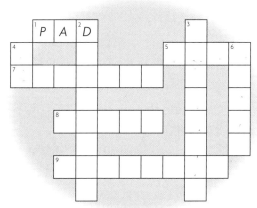

1 Communication

1 Grammar

✻ Past simple vs. present perfect simple

a Complete the dialogues. Use the past simple or the present perfect simple form of the verbs.

1 Anton: ____*Have*____ you two ____*met*____ (meet) before?

Lauren: Yes. We both ____*went*____ (go) to that party last week.

2 Setsuko: How long _____ you _____ (know) Marek?

Andrej: We _____ (meet) on the first day of this course.

3 Callum: _____ you _____ (see) any films last weekend?

Shayla: No. I _____ (not go) to the cinema for ages.

4 Ramon: _____ you _____ (finish) that Harry Potter book yet?

Tessa: Oh, yes, I _____ (take) it back to the library yesterday.

5 Jay: _____ you _____ (speak) to Will yesterday?

Soraya: No, I _____ (not see) him for a couple of days.

6 Carrie: _____ you _____ (buy) Lee's birthday present yet?

Jen: Yes, I _____ (get) her something in town last night.

7 Shandra: When _____ you _____ (learn) to drive?

Jack: Me? I _____ (never drive) a car in my life.

b Complete the questions. Use the past simple or present perfect simple.

1 A: I've got really bad toothache.

B: Oh, I'm sorry. How long *have you had it* ?

2 A: We don't live in Hutton Avenue any more.

B: Oh, I didn't know that. When _____ ?

3 A: We had a great time at the cinema last night.

B: Oh, really? What film _____ ?

4 A: I lived in Japan when I was younger.

B: That's interesting. How long _____ there?

5 A: I'm working part-time in a restaurant.

B: Oh, yeah? When _____ ?

6 A: So you've finally arrived!

B: Sorry I'm late! How long _____ _____ here?

c Complete the sentences with the present simple, past simple and present perfect simple forms of the verbs.

1 I ____*know*____ Pete. I _____ him for years. In fact, our grandfathers _____ each other when they were alive. (know)

2 He _____ at this restaurant since last summer. He _____ in the kitchen. Before that, he _____ in a shop. (work)

3 When she was younger, she _____ in Russia. Now she _____ in Japan. She _____ there for five years. (live)

4 I _____ my leg. I _____ it on a skiing trip last month. I _____ something every time I ski. (break)

d Read the diary of a woman who went to a seminar to learn how to talk to animals. Some of the lines have a word that should not be there. Write the word at the end of the line, or tick (✔) if the line is correct.

I arrived here last night. Today we all paid our fee, $160 for an eight-hour	1	✔
workshop. Then we got to know our trainer, a woman is called Claire.	2	*is*
'I've had have horses since my childhood,' she said. 'But it took me a	3	....
long while to find out that I can understand them! You can to learn this too.	4	....
Animals talk all the time. You just need to learn to listen to them.' After	5	....
breakfast we have worked in pairs. 'Close your eyes, think of a message	6	....
and communicate it through your thoughts,' said Claire. I decided	7	....
to 'tell' to my partner that 'The mountain is purple.' After two minutes of	8	....
concentration (I got a headache) she told for me what she understood: 'It's	9	....
too hot in here!' Well, never mind, we're here to read the thoughts of	10	....
animals, not humans! After lunch, we did sat on the grass near Claire's	11	....
horses and closed our eyes. Half an hour since later we went back to the	12	....
house. So what messages did we have read? 'It's hot.' 'We like the grass.'	13	....
Do I really need an animal communicator to learn that a horses like grass?	14	....

✱ Time expressions

e Two time expressions are correct, and one is incorrect. ~~Cross out~~ the incorrect answer.

1 Have you called your mother *already / yet / ~~yesterday~~*?
2 Philip has *already / just* left school *in 2004*.
3 We didn't have time to clean up *last night / already / before* we left.
4 Actually, I saw that film *two days ago / just / on Sunday*.
5 They've *never* seen snow *last winter / already*.
6 I haven't heard from Mike *since the party / for a few days / about a week ago*.
7 We had an old black Beetle *when I was little / since the 80s / for about ten years*.

f Rewrite the sentences using the words in brackets.

1 I've known Mrs Craig for four years. (met)
   I met Mrs Craig four years ago.
2 Jessica bought her mobile phone last week. (for)
   ....
3 William called a minute ago. (just)
   ....
4 How long have you had that bag? (buy)
   ....
5 Your friends have been here for an hour. (ago)
   ....
6 Your birthday cards got here yesterday. (since)
   ....
7 The last time I saw you was at your party. (haven't)
   ....

2 Pronunciation

✱ Sentence stress

a Read the sentences. <u>Underline</u> the words that are stressed. Sometimes there is more than one possibility.

1 How long have you had it?
2 When did you move?
3 What film did you see?
4 How long did you live there?
5 When did you start working there?
6 How long have you been here?

b ▶ **CD3 T12** Listen, check and repeat.

3 Vocabulary

✱ Body language

a Match the two parts of the sentences. Write a–j in the boxes.

1	That guy's leaning	*i*	a	back in your chair and enjoy this film.
2	Could you try to make		b	you that warm smile when you walk in the room.
3	Just sit		c	your eyebrows at me? Is there a problem?
4	If you agree, nod		d	nervous, even if you feel it!
5	Just try to avoid		e	eye contact with the waiter? I need some water.
6	She's fantastic – she always gives		f	eye contact if you don't want to talk to him.
7	Try not to look		g	about? Do you think she's in trouble?
8	Did you just raise		h	your arms. I hope you're not getting impatient with me.
9	I see you've just folded		i	forward a lot – do you think he's trying to listen to us?
10	What do you think she's gesturing		j	your head three times.

✱ *say* and *tell*

b Complete the sentences with the correct form of *say* or *tell*.

1 I can't _____tell_____ the difference between the new version and the old one.

2 If something is bothering you, please _____ it out loud – don't whisper to your friends.

3 He's only two years old, but he can already _____ the time.

4 Can I _____ you a secret if you promise to keep it to yourself?

5 I hope you're not _____ me a lie. You'll be in trouble if you are.

6 I'm sure you've _____ me that joke before. Don't you know any others?

c Complete the sentences with the correct form of *say* or *tell* and one of the expressions in the box.

thank you   sorry   goodbye   a prayer   you off   him a story   the truth   that again

1 I've got a job interview this afternoon, so I need some luck. Will you _____*say a prayer*_____ ?

2 Ouch! That really hurt! Aren't you going to _____ ?

3 Sorry, I didn't hear you. Could you _____ ?

4 I don't believe you! Are you sure you're _____ ?

5 That's a really nice present your grandma sent you. You need to write and _____ .

6 He won't go to sleep until you _____ .

7 Well, that's the end of the class. It's time to _____ .

8 Look what you've done! Wait until your dad sees this – he's really going to _____ .

d (**Vocabulary bank**) Replace the underlined words with a phrase from the box. Write a–j in the boxes.

> **a** talks nonsense **b** talk back **c** speak a word of **d** on speaking terms **e** talk sport
> **f** Talk about **g** ~~spoke too soon~~ **h** Speak up **i** speak your mind **j** talking shop

1 Mum said it wasn't going to rain, but she said that without thinking. The sky's full of dark clouds. [g]

2 I can't hear a word you're saying. Talk more loudly, please. [ ]

3 Alex, don't reply rudely to the teacher like that! [ ]

4 I only spoke English when I was on holiday in Spain, because I can't say anything at all in Spanish. [ ]

5 I'd like you to tell me exactly what you think. [ ]

6 I don't want to go out with Tom and his friends – they just discuss things like football all the time. [ ]

7 You can't believe a word that Jason says. He says stupid things all the time! [ ]

8 I've just read this book. It's absolutely fantastic! You really must read it. [ ]

9 Dad loves discussing work with his colleagues. [ ]

10 Francesca and Ally have argued again. They aren't communicating with each other at all at the moment. [ ]

4 Culture in mind

Read the text. Then mark the statements *T* (true), *F* (false) or *N* (not enough information).

1 Africans used drumming before Europeans discovered the continent. [ ]

2 Slaves used drumming to send messages about their slave masters. [ ]

3 Slave masters encouraged the use of drumming. [ ]

4 Some drumming sounds a bit like speech. [ ]

5 Drumming communication differs from one country to another. [ ]

6 People add new words and phrases to the drumming 'language' all the time. [ ]

7 About half of all drum messages are misunderstood. [ ]

Talking Drums

In some parts of Africa, drums have been used for communication for hundreds of years. That was how, for example, tribes knew that European explorers were on their way – they heard the drum messages from miles away, long before the explorers actually appeared. At one time, drums were banned, because slaves were using them to send messages to each other. The slave masters couldn't understand the messages and were worried about what the slaves were 'saying', so they banned the use of the drums.

There are three types of drumming. One type uses rhythms to send a particular signal. A second type of drumming repeats the patterns of speech (i.e. it matches the rhythm of specific words or sentences). And the third type is more musical. None of the forms of drumming are proper languages. Indeed, there is no international drumming language at all. Drum communication is localised and quite limited. People can't suddenly add new expressions to the drumming, so it can't be used to say anything you want. And there is always a danger that messages will be misunderstood. Nevertheless, drumming is still a valuable way of sending limited information, where the people who hear it understand the message.

Skills in mind

5 Write

a Read this email to Laura from her friend Nadia.

> To: lauranichols@easymail.com
> From: n.stephens@dphigh.edu
>
> Hey girl! Just a quick email to tell you I'm still alive! Mum said I can't use my phone this month, 'cos I spent too much last month.
>
> Oh, well. Listen – email me back.
> – How's your week been?
> – Any luck with finding a job?
> – Things OK with Tom?
> – Ian Finch's party!! It's tomorrow night. Are we meeting there?
> – Any other news I should know about?
>
> Write back soon!
>
> Love, Nadia

b Read Laura's reply. Does she answer all of Nadia's questions? What is wrong with the underlined phrases?

c Replace the underlined phrases above with phrases a–f below. Write 1–6 in the boxes.

a Things are going well with Tom [3]

b So, about [ ]

c Hi Nadia, [ ]

d He's still not sure about [ ]

e Take care [ ]

f I don't really want to do that [ ]

WRITING TIP

Using appropriate language

When you write a letter or an email, it is very important to choose language that is appropriate for the reader.

- Think about who the letter is for. If it is someone you already know (a friend or a pen-friend, for example), then your language can be more simple and informal.

- Make sure you include all the information you are asked to include, in a natural way.

- When you learn new words and expressions, ask your teacher if they are formal or informal. If you learn the way to start a formal letter, also find out how to start a letter to a pen-friend, for example.

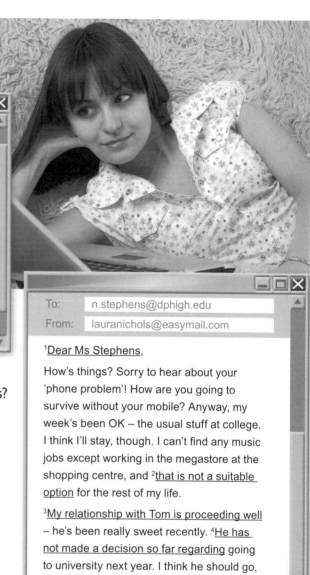

> To: n.stephens@dphigh.edu
> From: lauranichols@easymail.com
>
> [1]Dear Ms Stephens,
>
> How's things? Sorry to hear about your 'phone problem'! How are you going to survive without your mobile? Anyway, my week's been OK – the usual stuff at college. I think I'll stay, though. I can't find any music jobs except working in the megastore at the shopping centre, and [2]that is not a suitable option for the rest of my life.
>
> [3]My relationship with Tom is proceeding well – he's been really sweet recently. [4]He has not made a decision so far regarding going to university next year. I think he should go, even if it means we'll be apart. Decisions, decisions!
>
> [5]With reference to Ian's party – we could meet up before, if you want. How about Starblast Coffee at 7.30?
>
> Guess who we bumped into today? Ben Davis – he's back from Hong Kong. He seems a bit unhappy – his parents have broken up and he's not sure what he wants to do. He's coming to the party. You used to like Ben, didn't you?
>
> [6]Yours faithfully,
>
> Love Laura

d Write a similar 120-word email from Rebecca to Kylie in which she passes on her latest news using the information from Exercise 12 on page 7 of the Student's Book.

Unit check

1 Fill in the spaces

Complete the text with the words in the box.

> back   nod   make   ~~gesturing~~   telling   eye   forward   warm   look   arms

It's funny how different people communicate in groups. Some people are always *gesturing* with their hands, and others just stand with their ¹_____ folded. Some talk non-stop, and others just sit ²_____ and ³_____ their heads occasionally. I have a problem with people who don't ⁴_____ eye contact. When someone doesn't look at you, it looks like they're ⁵_____ lies, especially when they ⁶_____ nervous too. It's funny – you can give someone a ⁷_____ smile, but they still avoid ⁸_____ contact. It makes me want to lean ⁹_____ and say, 'Hey, it's me, I'm talking to you!'

| 9 |

2 Choose the correct answers

Circle the correct answer: a, b or c.

1 I've _____ made a terrible mistake.
   a yet   b ever   c (just)

2 She _____ seen her boyfriend all week.
   a never   b didn't   c hasn't

3 I _____ run to college in the mornings – it's only two kilometres.
   a haven't   b usually   c didn't

4 Wait! I haven't had breakfast _____ .
   a still   b ago   c yet

5 How long _____ you wait for me last night?
   a did   b have   c do

6 I can't believe your mum didn't _____ off for taking the car without asking.
   a say you   b tell   c tell you

7 My birthday was three days _____ .
   a ago   b just   c last

8 My brother and sister _____ bought me a present for my birthday.
   a didn't yet   b has never   c still haven't

9 You haven't _____ sorry for shouting at me.
   a say   b saying   c said

| 8 |

3 Vocabulary

Choose the correct word.

Our parents have always encouraged us to speak our ¹_____ . But that doesn't mean they want us to talk ²_____ . They ³_____ right away if we ever do that, and they tell us ⁴_____ for doing it. They don't like it if we talk ⁵_____ to them, either. Mum tried to give my brother a ⁶_____ about that the other day but he ⁷_____ off into his room, so he got away that time! Mum says good manners are important. We have to say 'please' and 'thank you', and we have to say it out ⁸_____ so everyone hears us.

1	a	words	b	minds	c	memories	d	voices
2	a	nonsense	b	lies	c	truth	d	silly
3	a	believe	b	reply	c	tell	d	notice
4	a	in	b	out	c	off	d	up
5	a	from	b	to	c	at	d	back
6	a	sign	b	warning	c	telling	d	saying
7	a	charged	b	ranged	c	signed	d	hid
8	a	noisy	b	wide	c	loud	d	big

| 8 |

How did you do?

Total: | 25 |

| ☺ Very good 20 – 25 | ☺ OK 14 – 19 | ☹ Review Unit 1 again 0 – 13 |

2 A true friend

1 Grammar

✱ Past simple vs. past continuous review

a Complete the sentences with the past simple or past continuous form of the verbs.

1 While I ___was looking___ (look) for my tennis balls, I ___found___ (find) an old sandwich under my bed.

2 When my parents _____ (come) back, we _____ (have) a party.

3 When I _____ (open) the door, they _____ (dance) in the dark.

4 I _____ (find) this girl's phone number while I _____ (clean) your room.

5 While we _____ (wait), we _____ (start) to write the invitations.

6 I _____ (teach) a gym class when I _____ (hear) about the plane crash.

7 Someone _____ (call) you on your mobile while you _____ (take) the dog for a walk.

b Complete the sentences with the past simple or past continuous form of the verbs.

Godzilla the cat had a special relationship with her owner, David Hart. David often ___went___ (go) away for work. While he [1] _____ (travel), his mother [2] _____ (come) over to his house to look after the cat. One day while the telephone [3] _____ (ring), his mother [4] _____ (notice) Godzilla get up off the sofa and sit down next to the phone. She [5] _____ (pick) up the phone. It was David. The next time the phone [6] _____ (ring), Godzilla [7] _____ (do) the same thing. It was David again. But the next time, Godzilla [8] _____ (not move). His mother [9] _____ (answer) the phone – it wasn't David. She started to notice that every time David

[10] _____ (phone), Godzilla [11] _____ (go) to sit next to the phone. When it wasn't David, Godzilla [12] _____ (stay) where she was.

✱ Time conjunctions: as / then / as soon as

c Connect the sentences with the words in brackets. Sometimes you need to change the order of the sentences.

1 His parents came to stay at his house. David went away to work. (when)
   When David went away to work, his
   parents came to stay at his house.

2 The phone started ringing. Godzilla ran and sat next to the phone. (as soon as)
   _____
   _____

3 The hall light came on. She was parking her car. (as)
   _____
   _____

4 The dog started barking. I got to the gate. (as soon as)
   _____
   _____

5 Sometimes an animal starts behaving strangely. Something happens to its owner. (then)
   _____
   _____

6 Many animals are waiting at the door. Their owners are still travelling home. (as)
   _____
   _____

2 Pronunciation

✱ Linking sounds

a Look at the way these words from Exercise 1b are linked:

her ⌣ owner   David ⌣ often
went ⌣ away   look ⌣ after

b ▶ CD3 T13 Mark similar links in the text, then listen and check.

3 Grammar

✱ Past simple vs. past perfect simple

a Match the sentence halves. Write a–d in the boxes.

1 A man was arrested for a bank robbery after police called him on his mobile phone. The man …

2 A man was arrested in hospital for trying to steal money from a house safe after police found his glove at the house. The safe …

3 A man who had climbed Mount Everest six times died as a result of a fall at home. He …

4 An unemployed man who tried to print his own money was caught as soon as he tried to spend it. He …

a had used black ink on the notes instead of green, because he was colour-blind.

b had left a business card at the bank with his phone number on it.

c had fallen on his hand and cut off one of his fingers. The man ran away, leaving his glove behind. When the man went to hospital with a missing finger, the police were able to match the finger to the hand.

d had climbed a ladder to change a light bulb in the kitchen when he fell and cracked his head on the sink.

b Complete the sentences. Use the past perfect and the past simple or past continuous form of the verbs.

1 As soon as he ___closed___ (close) the door, he _____ (realise) that he _____ (leave) his key inside.

2 I _____ (have) the feeling that I _____ (meet) her somewhere before.

3 I _____ (not know) what I _____ (say) to her, but she _____ (cry).

4 They _____ (get) to the cinema ten minutes after the film _____ (start).

5 My mobile _____ (not work) because I _____ (forget) to charge it.

6 I _____ (see) you sitting and smiling half an hour before the end of the exam. _____ you already _____ (finish)?

c Read the text about the American TV show *Friends*. Some of the lines have a word that should not be there. The extra words are connected to tenses. Write the incorrect extra word at the end of the line, or tick (✔) if the line is correct.

Friends is still ~~being~~ one of the most popular TV shows in the world,	1 ____being____
even after they stopped making it in 2004. The show had had three	2 ____✔____
previous names before it had became simply *Friends*: *Friends Like Us*,	3 _____
Across The Hall and *Six Of One*, but in the end one word was been	4 _____
enough. Apart from the six main characters, the only other person to	5 _____
appear in all ten years that they have made the show was Gunther, the	6 _____
coffee shop server. He was having the only person in the cast that knew	7 _____
how to operate a cappuccino machine.	
Why was the show so popular? It was being usually well written and	8 _____
funny, of course, but what has kept fans watching for more than a decade	9 _____
is possibly the fact that the group of six always did stayed friends, no	10 _____
matter what were problems the characters had on screen, or the actors	11 _____
had in real life.	

4 Vocabulary

✴ Friends and enemies

a Replace the <u>underlined</u> words with a phrase from the box. Write a–f in the boxes.

> a let me down   b fallen out   c ~~tell on me~~   d stand by you   e get on well with
> f sticking up for me

1 Please don't <u>tell anyone that I did it</u>! I'll be your friend forever! `c`

2 Your most loyal friends are the ones who <u>stay loyal to you</u> in the bad times. ☐

3 Thanks for <u>supporting me</u> in there. I thought nobody was going to agree with me. ☐

4 You really <u>have a good relationship with</u> your stepbrothers and stepsisters, don't you? ☐

5 It looks like Darren and Varsha have <u>stopped being friends</u>. They don't talk to each other any more. ☐

6 You said you would go with me! Please don't <u>disappoint me</u> – I don't want to go alone. ☐

b Look at the pictures. Choose a phrase from the box in Exercise 4a to complete sentences 1–5 below. There is one phrase you won't need.

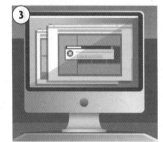

1 Oh, no! What have I done? Look, don't ___c___ and I'll give you some of my sweets.

2 It's amazing that they _____ each other.

3 Come on, come on! Please don't _____ now!

4 Phew! Thanks for _____ .

5 Oh, no! It looks like they've _____ with each other. Be careful what you say.

c **Vocabulary bank** Complete the sentences with the words in the box.

> allies   acquaintance   ~~old~~   hit it off
> mate   make   friends are for   close

1 I've known Arthur for a very long time – we're ___old___ friends.

2 The two countries were _____ during the war.

3 He's very shy – it isn't easy for him to _____ friends with people.

4 We met, he liked me and I liked him – we _____ immediately!

5 They know all of each other's secrets and so on – they're really _____ friends.

6 This is Alex – he's a _____ of mine from our school days.

7 She isn't a friend really, just a business _____ of my mother's.

8 You don't have to thank me – that's what _____ , after all.

⑤ Everyday English

ⓐ Complete the expressions with the words in the box.

> then   could   ~~especially~~   sooner   news   matter

1   A: Do you like Chinese food?

    B: Not _especially_ .

2   A: Dan hasn't invited you to his party.

    B: Well, I won't invite him to mine,
       _____ .

3   A: Do you mind if I copy your homework?

    B: As a _____ of fact I do. Do it
       yourself.

4   A: Are you going to Diana's party?

    B: Party? That's _____ to me. I didn't know
       she was having one.

5   A: Mum, I'm sorry. I ate the last piece of cake.

    B: How _____ you? I was saving that for
       your dad.

6   A: When do you want our homework in, Sir?

    B: The _____ the better, but no later than
       Thursday.

ⓑ Complete the dialogue with the expressions from Exercise 5a.

Steve: Hey Brian, do you like MGMT?

Brian: [1] ___Not especially___ , why?

Steve: They're playing at the Academy in May.

Brian: Really? [2] _____ . Are you going?

Steve: Absolutely. I bought my tickets yesterday.

Brian: Tickets?

Steve: Yes, one's for Jen. I've invited her along.

Brian: What! [3] _____ ? You know I like her.

Steve: So why don't you come along, [4] _____ ?

Brian: [5] _____ I think I will. When should I get my
         ticket?

Steve: [6] _____ . They're selling really quickly.

Brian: OK, I'm going to buy mine now! See you.

⑥ Study help

✳ Using appropriate language

- When you learn new words and phrases, it is important to know if the language is formal or informal. For example, it is not appropriate to end a letter requesting information about a course with 'Take care'. At the same time, you can sound too formal if you write 'Yours faithfully' in an email to someone you met on a school exchange programme.

- Phrasal verbs are usually, but not always, more informal ways of saying something. It is fine to say to a friend 'Let's meet up sometime', but in a formal situation it would be better to say 'I would like to arrange an appointment for ...'.

Skills in mind

7 Listen

a ▶ CD3 T14 Read statements A–C below, then listen and read what the person says about pets and their owners. Decide which statement you think is the speaker's opinion.

A Pet owners have a special understanding with their animals.

B Only dogs have a telepathic relationship with their owners, not other pets.

C The 'special relationship' between a pet and its owner does not really exist.

'A lot of people seem to think that pets, especially dogs, are somehow telepathic. They think that they have a special understanding with their animal, so that for example, their pet knows when they are coming home, or knows when something is wrong. I think that's ridiculous, though. These things are just coincidence, or it's just that the owner is trying to 'wish' that their pet is special.'

The speaker says 'A lot of people seem to think …', but this probably does not include the speaker. The speaker also says 'especially dogs', which does not mean only dogs. The third and fourth sentences give the speaker's opinion: 'I think …'. The correct answer is 'C'.

LISTENING TIP

Matching speakers with opinions

- In this kind of question, you will usually hear a number of different people talking about a similar subject.

- It is important to read the statements carefully first, to be clear about the differences between each one.

- The speakers may use different words from the ones in the statements, but the meaning will be the same.

- Try to think of other ways to express the ideas in the statements, to imagine what the speaker might say. For example, when the statement is 'It's not necessary', the speaker might say 'You don't have to' or 'You don't need to'.

- The speaker may seem to be agreeing with the statement because they use the same words, but actually go on to disagree with the statement and therefore think the opposite. For example, the speaker might say, '*Some people* think you have to see your best friend every day, *but I don't* think that's necessary.'

- Remember you are being asked for *the speaker's* opinion, not yours!

b ▶ CD3 T15 Listen to five people talking about best friends, and match each speaker with one of the options A–F. Use each letter only once. There is one extra letter you won't need.

Speaker 1 ☐   A It's not necessary to see your best friend every day.

Speaker 2 ☐   B You don't always like people the first time you meet them.

Speaker 3 ☐   C Some people don't have any friends.

Speaker 4 ☐   D It's not important to have a 'best' friend.

Speaker 5 ☐   E It's not so hard to make 'new best friends'.

F It's normal to fight with your best friend sometimes.

Unit check

1 Fill in the spaces

Complete the text with the words in the box.

> loyalty ~~friendships~~ up out stood get letting had while friends

One of the great ___*friendships*___ in literature is the one between the hobbits Frodo Baggins and Samwise Gamgee in *The Lord of the Rings*. Sam, who [1] _____ been Frodo's servant at their home in the Shire, accompanied Frodo and his company on a journey to destroy the ring and save the world. [2] _____ they were making their journey, Sam [3] _____ by his master through all kinds of danger, never [4] _____ him down. The story shows us that, even for people who [5] _____ on very well, there are times when our [6] _____ is tested and we can fall [7] _____ with each other. However, true [8] _____ always stick [9] _____ for each other in the end.

| 9 |

2 Choose the correct answers

(Circle) the correct answer: a, b or c.

1 You're not going to tell _____ her, are you?
   a well   b down   c (on)

2 Her old car never _____ her down.
   a makes   b does   c lets

3 _____ soon as we left, the snow started.
   a While   b As   c Then

4 I _____ already bought my tickets for the show before we got to the theatre.
   a have   b was   c had

5 Dogs are very _____ to their owners.
   a loyal   b friend   c stick

6 While she was having a shower, somebody _____ her towel.
   a stole   b had stolen   c was stealing

7 _____ my brother was born, we moved to a bigger house.
   a While   b When   c Then

8 My best friend and I fall _____ about twice a week, but we're soon friends again.
   a up   b out   c in

9 I _____ want to watch the film because I had seen it three times before.
   a hadn't   b didn't   c wasn't

| 8 |

3 Vocabulary

(Circle) the correct words.

1 A good friend will always stand *on* / (*by*) you, no matter what.

2 I think it's great the way you stick *up* / *out* for your friend.

3 He's not really a friend but more of a/an *acquaintance* / *mate* – someone I knew at school.

4 I get *on* / *up* really well with all my teachers. I really like them.

5 Ali and I *hit* / *fell* it off as soon as we met. We've been friends ever since.

6 She's a really *close* / *open* friend. I tell her everything.

7 You don't need to thank me. That's *why* / *what* friends are for.

8 She feels you really *let* / *threw* her down. That's why's she's upset with you.

9 If you hit me again I'm going to tell *on* / *out* you to the teacher.

| 8 |

How did you do?

Total: | 25 |

| Very good 20 – 25 | 😐 OK 14 – 19 | ☹ Review Unit 2 again 0 – 13 |

3 A working life

1 Grammar

✱ Present perfect simple vs. continuous review

a Circle the correct words.

1 Your brother has (written) / *been writing* three job applications this morning.

2 I've *been doing / done* an IT course at the weekends. I've got one more week to go.

3 I don't leave school for another year, but I've already *started / been starting* to look for a job.

4 Have you *seen / been seeing* the new James Bond film?

5 My dad has always *had / been having* a thick beard.

6 What do you mean, you haven't had time to make dinner! What have you *done / been doing* all evening?

7 It's *snowed / been snowing* all night. Do you think it'll stop by tomorrow morning?

b Complete the sentences with the words in the box.

gone   ~~been going~~   called   been calling
taken   been taking   painted   been painting

1 Her French is getting much better. She's _been going_ to classes twice a week.

2 I've _____ three of the walls and both doors – just one more wall to go.

3 You've just _____ me! Did you forget to tell me something?

4 He's _____ out, I'm afraid. If you want to wait, he'll be back in an hour.

5 I've _____ photos for the last two hours. The camera doesn't have any memory left now.

6 Have you _____ in here? It certainly smells like it.

7 Alisha's _____ you all day. Where have you been?

8 Who has _____ the last piece of cake? I wanted it!

c Match the dialogues and pictures, then complete. Use the present perfect simple or continuous.

1 A: Where's your sister?
   B: She ___'s gone___ out with her friend. (go)

2 A: You look terrible! What's wrong?
   B: Oh, I _____ (not sleep) well recently. Too much homework, I think!

3 A: Do you want another slice of this pizza? It's excellent.
   B: No, thanks. I _____ enough. (eat)

4 A: I'm so sorry I'm late! How long _____ you _____ ? (wait)
   B: Too long! I'm soaking wet.

5 A: What _____ you _____ ? (do)
   B: Helping Dad change a tyre on the car.

6 A: _____ you _____ (finish) the washing-up in there?
   B: No, not yet. _____ you _____ (see) how many dirty dishes there are?

d Complete the questions. Use the present perfect simple or continuous form of the verbs in the box.

do   have   ~~go~~   download   save   know

1 So is that your new boyfriend? How long
  have you been going out with him?

2 Nice phone, Jake. How long ....
  it?

3 I didn't know you could water ski! How long
  .... that?

4 I hear you want to buy a new sound system.
  How long .... for it?

5 You didn't tell me you'd passed all of your
  exams! How long .... ?

6 That film file is huge! How long
  .... it?

e Continue the biography of singer/songwriter Craig David using the information below. Use past simple and present perfect simple or continuous where appropriate.

- born in Southampton, England (1981)
- started singing and DJing at age 14
- youngest ever male singer to have a UK number 1 hit (April, 2000)
- won various music industry awards since then
- also recorded his song *Rise And Fall* in Punjabi
- met Nelson Mandela
- called "England's best singer" by Sir Elton John
- played many charity concerts and football matches
- received honorary Doctor of Music degree from Southampton University (2008)

Craig David was born in 1981 in Southampton, England. He has been singing and DJing...

2 Grammar

⭐ *had better / should / ought to*

a Circle the correct words in these sentences.

a You'd better / should / ought do it before Mum comes home!

b You oughtn't / better not / shouldn't play with matches.

c You ought not / better not / shouldn't to let him use the internet at night.

d You better / should / ought talk to some of your teachers about it.

e You'd should / better / ought wear some smart clothes. You need to look your best!

f You ought / should / better to look at the advertisements in the paper.

b Match the problems below with the advice in Exercise 2a. Write the letters a–g in the boxes.

1 'My son spends all night in chat rooms.' [c]

2 'I've burnt my fingers.' [ ]

3 'I want a good part-time job.' [ ]

4 'I've got a job interview tomorrow.' [ ]

5 'I don't know what career I want.' [ ]

6 'I haven't tidied up my bedroom yet.' [ ]

3 Pronunciation

⭐ /ɔː/ *short*

a There are fourteen words on this page that have the sound /ɔː/. Can you find them all? Don't repeat the same word, and don't include *for* (because this has the sound /fə/).

b ▶CD3 T16 Listen to the fourteen words, and repeat.

4 Vocabulary

✱ Jobs and work

a Complete the crossword by solving the clues with words from page 29 of the Student's Book.

Across

4 Not working all of the working week (4-4)

7 You have this if you've done the job before (10)

9 Working the complete week (4-4)

10 Leave a job (6)

11 This is your money from work (6)

Down

1 A worker for a company (8)

2 You can get them from school and university (14)

3 Without a job (10)

5 Someone who is learning the skills of a job (7)

6 Try to get a job (5)

8 The person/employer you work for (8)

b Complete the two dialogues with words from the box.

> salary   ~~qualifications~~   applied   employer   employees

Interviewer: Well, Ms Lane, I see you have 10 GCSEs, and six of them with an A grade. Those are very impressive *qualifications* . Why have you ¹ _____ for a job with us?

Ms Lane: I think you're a very fair ² _____ . You treat your ³ _____ very well from what I hear. And the ⁴ _____ is excellent for a first job.

> ~~full-time~~   part-time   resigned   trainee   unemployed

Job Shop Officer: Are you in _____*full-time*_____ work at the moment, Alan?

Alan: No, I'm not working at all. I've been ¹ _____ for the last two weeks.

Job Shop Officer: I see you ² _____ from your previous job in your first month as a ³ _____ . What happened?

Alan: The training programme was very poor. I wanted to find something better.

Job Shop Officer: I see. Well, we only have ⁴ _____ jobs in your field at the moment – mornings, Monday to Friday, 20 hours a week. Would that interest you?

The crossword (partially filled):

4 P A R 5T T I M E

✱ Fields of work

c Match the jobs 1–8 with the fields of work. Add more jobs if you can.

a public service _____5,_____

b education _____

c entertainment _____

d health care _____

e IT and media _____

f legal _____

g finance _____

h management _____

5 Fiction in mind

a While you read the extract, choose the best word to complete the gaps.

1 a computer   b (secretary)   c manager

2 a away   b about   c around

3 a Maybe   b However   c If

4 a work   b worked   c working

5 a told   b said   c spoke

You are going to read more of 'The Book of Thoughts'. Chester has discovered that the old book he found in the antique shop really does tell him what other people are thinking. But will this help him at work?

Chester walked into his office. His [1] _secretary_ was already busy typing.

'Any messages, Miss Han?' he asked her.

'Yes, Sir,' said Miss Han, 'from the Manager. He says he can't go the meeting today about the Eastern business. He wants you to take over right [2] _____.'

Yes!

This was the kind of opportunity he'd been waiting for. He would show them all just how good he was. This was an important piece of business. [3] _____ he could make sure that everything went well he would get noticed. He would be an obvious choice for the next manager's job. If he became a manager he would be the youngest manager in the business! [...]

When he met the others Chester was confident and did his job well. He made sure that everybody knew what to do. The meeting that afternoon was sure to be a success. If, of course, the figures he had were all correct.

Just then he noticed a little smile on the face of Mr Shaw. 'What's the old man got to smile about?' thought Chester. 'He never smiles – why is he smiling now?' Then he remembered his little book.

He took it out of his pocket and hid it behind some papers. He pretended to be looking at his notes and thought of Mr Shaw. The words appeared immediately:

I'll teach that young fool a lesson. I've got some figures he doesn't know about hidden in my office. I've been [4] _____ on this longer than he has. When he can't come up with the right figures, he'll look stupid. Then I'll produce them and save the day. He'll look like a boy trying to do a man's job. He needs to learn some respect for serious professionals like me.

Chester felt a cold sweat on the back of his neck.

'So the old man really does dislike me, after all!'

Chester wondered what all the others thought about him but had no time to consult his book.

'Thanks everybody – see you all this afternoon', Chester [5] _____ them all. 'Enjoy your lunch.'

(from Brennan, F. (2000) 'The Book of Thoughts' in *The Fruitcake Special*, CUP: pp 56–57)

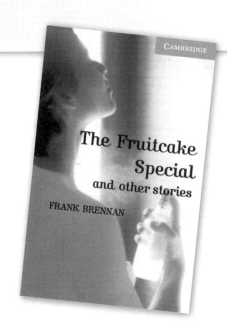

b Choose the correct answer: a, b, c or d.

1 Why is Chester so pleased at his secretary's news?

  a He'll have the chance to take some time off.

  b He'll be able to work more closely with Mr Shaw.

  c He'll have the chance to earn his manager's respect.

  d He'll be able to find out what his work colleagues think of him.

2 Why does Chester use the little book?

  a To check his figures for the meeting.

  b To read Mr Shaw's thoughts.

  c To write what he thinks about the office employees.

  d To hide his figures from Mr Shaw.

3 How does Chester feel at the end of the extract?

  a cold   b uncomfortable   c cheerful   d hungry

6 Listen and write

a ▶CD3 T17 Listen to Chris describing a concert he saw, and complete the missing information 1–7.

b Match the <u>underlined</u> words and phrases a–d in the text with phrases 1–4.

1 all in all ☐

2 in conclusion ☐

3 was held ☐

4 well worth it ☐

WRITING TIP

Report writing

A report is similar to a description or review. It is normally written in a clear, semi-formal style, divided into paragraphs with headings to show what kind of information the reader will find. The report usually ends with a recommendation, which may contain your opinion.

● It helps to use headings for your paragraphs. You can then plan what you want to write, and your report will be easier to read.

● Try to learn useful words and expressions such as those underlined in the report and in Exercise 6b.

● Try to present your information as factually as you can, leaving your main opinions for the conclusion.

● In your conclusion, give a balanced assessment if possible. Be careful not to repeat what you wrote in previous paragraphs. If you are saying that you did not like something, try to find something positive to say.

Introduction

This report will describe a live event I attended recently. The event was a pop concert featuring [1] _____ten_____ different singers and bands. Some of the money from [2] _____ sales was given to charity, for people with physical and mental disabilities.

Venue and cost

The concert [a] <u>took place</u> at the M.E.N. Arena in Manchester. Tickets were [3] _____ , depending on where the seats were.

Atmosphere

At the beginning of the show, the sound wasn't [4] _____ . Later, the quality improved a lot. The lighting was very impressive. The crowd was very young; the average age was probably about [5] _____ .

Performances

Most of the performers played [6] _____ songs. There were some delays between performances. The Black Eyed Peas were the main band; they played last. I thought Lady Gaga was the best performer; her singing and dancing were excellent, and the audience responded very well.

Conclusion

[b] <u>To sum up</u>, the show was [7] _____ long, which was [c] <u>good value for money</u>. Not all performers were equally good, though, and perhaps it would be a good idea to cut the number of performers. This show is touring the country, and my recommendation is that, if you like just two or three of the artists, you should definitely go and see it. [d] <u>Overall</u>, it was an excellent evening, with something for everyone.

c Your class is doing a survey on live events that they have attended (music concerts, dance and theatre performances, craft fairs, sports, etc.). Write a report of 120–150 words about a live event you have seen, including:

● where the event was held

● the cost

● a general description

● what you liked/didn't like

● whether other people might like it

● a recommendation as to how it could be better

Unit check

1 Fill in the spaces

Complete the text with the words in the box.

| part-time | for | should | been | working | job | qualifications | experience | trainee | employee |

Everybody keeps asking me what kind of ....job........ I want to do when I leave school. My mum doesn't think I [1] .... apply [2] .... any jobs yet. She wants me to go to university and get some good [3] .... so that I can be a teacher. My dad wants me to start [4] .... for his bank as a(n) [5] .... He says I could do the job [6] .... to get some [7] .... , and go to college on my days off. I don't know if I want to be a(n) [8] .... of a bank, though. I've [9] .... thinking about maybe trying to sell some of my art. Decisions, decisions!

☐ 9

2 Choose the correct answers

(Circle) the correct answer: a, b or c.

1 How long have you been .... ?
   a resigning b (unemployed) c experienced

2 I really think you'd .... say sorry before it's too late.
   a should b ought c better

3 How long have you .... waiting for me?
   a just b had c been

4 Why don't you .... for that job? You might get it.
   a apply b trainee c employee

5 .... she be doing that?
   a Has b Should c Had

6 It looks like she .... been crying.
   a has b just c have

7 She's a good .... and I like working for her.
   a employee b women c employer

8 I didn't get the job as I don't have enough work ....
   a trainee b experience c qualification

9 When do you think we .... to tell them we're leaving?
   a ought b should c better

☐ 8

3 Vocabulary

Match the two parts of sentences. Write a–i in the boxes.

1 Volunteering is a good way ☐ g
2 If you don't like your job, ☐
3 You should apply ☐
4 If you like, I'll help you fill ☐
5 Good qualifications will help ☐
6 There are other jobs in education ☐
7 The entertainment field is more ☐
8 I'd rather have my own business ☐
9 Studying law is a good way ☐

a apart from teaching.
b in the application form.
c in to the legal field.
d you to get a good job.
e maybe you should resign.
f for a job in IT.
g to get some experience.
h than just acting and singing.
i than be somebody's employee.

☐ 8

How did you do?

Total: ☐ 25

| :) | Very good 20 – 25 | :| | OK 14 – 19 | :(| Review Unit 3 again 0 – 13 |

4 Live forever!

1 Grammar

✱ Future predictions

a Complete the sentences with the correct form of *(not) be likely to*.

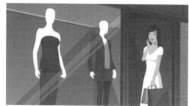

1 'It's nice, but it _____'s likely_____ _____to_____ be really expensive.'

2 'Please write it down, because I _____ forget.'

3 'You _____ fail the exam.'

4 'He _____ play again for about six months.'

5 'I _____ pass, am I?'

6 'Perhaps we shouldn't play here – we _____ break something.'

b Complete the sentences. Use the information in the chart.

100%	will	
75%	will probably	be likely to
50%	might	might not
25%	probably won't	not be likely to
0%	won't	

1 It / rain at the weekend. (75% + *will*)
   It will probably rain at the weekend.

2 My parents / be unhappy with my results. (100%)
   ----

3 My brother / arrive late tomorrow. (75% + *likely*)
   ----

4 The match on Saturday / be very good. (0%)
   ----

5 I / go to the cinema this evening. (50%)
   ----

6 I / pass next week's test. (75% + *likely*)
   ----

7 They / be at home tomorrow. (25% + *not likely*)
   ----

8 There / be much to eat at the party. (25% + *won't*)
   ----

9 We / visit our grandparents next weekend. (50% + *not*)
   ----

c Rewrite the sentences. Use the words in brackets.

1 The chances of my father buying me a computer are small. (likely)
   My father isn't likely to buy me a computer.

2 It's possible that I will pass the exams. (might)
   ----

3 It's possible that he won't arrive on time. (might not)
   ----

4 I'm almost sure that I'll be late. (probably)
   ----

5 There is a small chance my mother will lend me some money. (not likely)
   ----

6 I don't think that my sister will buy that car. (probably won't)

....

7 It's very possible that they will be at the party. (likely)

....

2 Grammar

✱ First conditional review: *if* and *unless*

a Complete the sentences with the present simple form of the verbs, or *will/won't*.

1 I ____*will lend*____ (lend) you the money if you ____*promise*____ (promise) to give it back tomorrow.

2 If she .... (phone) me tonight, I .... (ask) her to go out with me.

3 The door .... (not open) unless you .... (push) it hard.

4 Unless we .... (leave) now, we .... (be) late for school.

5 If he .... (not be) careful, he .... (hurt) himself.

6 I .... (not come) if you .... (not want) me to.

7 Unless you .... (stop) talking, the teacher .... (get) angry with you.

8 The dog .... (not bite) you if you .... (leave) it alone.

b Make conditional sentences with the words below.

1 you / have an accident / unless / you go more slowly

You'll have an accident unless you go more slowly.

2 If / John / invite me to the party, / I / go

....

3 I / beat Sally / unless / I / play badly

....

4 I / be very upset / if / he / lose my camera

....

5 Unless / you / go now, / the shops / be closed

....

6 If / my friend / come round, / we / play computer games

....

3 Grammar

✱ Time conjunctions: *if / unless / when / until / as soon as*

a Circle the correct words.

1 I'll tell you *until /* (as soon as) I know.

2 Mary isn't here yet so let's wait *until / when* she arrives.

3 I'm going to buy a new computer *when / unless* I have enough money.

4 You won't pass the exams *if / unless* you study more.

5 We'll go out *as soon as / unless* the weather gets better.

6 I'll stay at home *as soon as / until* it stops raining.

7 *When / Unless* we move house, I'll have my own bedroom.

8 *If / Until* I fail my driving test, I'll take it again.

b Complete the sentences. Use *if, unless, until* or *as soon as*.

1 She's coming home at 6.00. I'll talk to her ____*as soon as*____ she arrives.

2 .... we hurry up, we'll be late for the film!

3 Dad's picking us up in the car, so we'll have to wait .... he gets here.

4 What will you do .... you don't pass your exams?

5 Can you do me a favour? Look after my cat .... I get back from holiday, please.

6 I can't buy it .... my parents lend me some money.

7 I can't talk now, I'm watching a football match – but I'll ring you .... it finishes, OK?

8 .... the cinema's full, don't worry – we can come back home and watch a video.

4 Vocabulary

✱ Verbs with prepositions

a Find five words in the grid to complete the phrases.

G	A	R	G	E	T	T	I	N	G
R	R	E	O	V	T	H	N	E	R
O	G	A	R	R	H	I	R	A	E
W	O	R	R	Y	I	N	G	R	V
O	I	N	A	N	N	K	O	N	I
R	V	I	S	I	K	O	I	I	S
I	W	N	K	G	I	N	N	G	I
A	R	G	U	I	N	G	G	T	N
N	Y	R	R	I	G	O	I	R	G
G	E	T	T	T	I	N	G	S	W

Common causes of stress:

1 _____ with people

2 _____ about your problems

3 _____ for exams

4 _____ about what to wear

5 _____ ready for school

b Look at the pictures. Complete the sentences with the expressions from Exercise 4a.

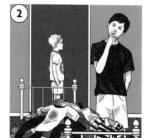

1 I hate ___getting ready___ for school! I almost always forget a book or something.

2 My brother's going to a party tonight, and he's spent hours _____ .

3 I think _____ is pointless! Either you've learned the things already, or you haven't!

4 Don't sit there _____ – go and do something about them!

5 He's a really unpleasant guy – he's always _____ and fighting.

c Complete the sentences with the correct prepositions.

1 I'm a bit worried ___about___ my sister.

2 My parents are thinking _____ moving to another town.

3 School ends next week, so I'm getting ready _____ the summer holidays.

4 Which exam are you revising _____ ?

5 Why are you always arguing _____ your parents?

6 What are you waiting _____ ?

5 Pronunciation

✱ Weak and strong forms of prepositions

▶CD3 T18 Listen and repeat. Pay particular attention to the underlined words.

1 I'm looking <u>for</u> my books.

2 What are you waiting <u>for</u>?

3 Sorry – I don't want to talk <u>to</u> you.

4 Who are you writing <u>to</u>?

5 Are you looking <u>at</u> me?

6 Who are you looking <u>at</u>?

6 **Vocabulary bank** Complete the cartoons with the correct prepositions.

1 "I'd like to apply __for__ the job of bank manager."

2 "My son doesn't like some of the parents I go round _____ ."

3 "I don't think I'll go _____ dessert, thanks."

4 "We can only hope _____ someone to find us soon."

5 "Do you think they'll have anything to talk _____ ?"

6 "We'll probably be able to laugh _____ it one day."

7 Study help

✱ Learning and recording words in context

- It's very important to record words that you learn in a context – in other words, don't record them as words on their own.

- For example: if you learn the verb 'worry', you <u>could</u> record it as one word and then write a translation, e.g. 'worry = *preocuparse*'.

- But in order to <u>use</u> the word 'worry', you need to know and remember words that go with it – e.g. the preposition 'about'. So it's

much better to write a sentence or phrase that uses the other words too, e.g. 'She never seems to worry about anything'. (You can add a translation if you think it's important and useful.)

- It's also a good idea to record <u>your own</u> sentences/phrases, about things which are true for you – this makes new language much more memorable.

Write sentences/phrases in your notebook (or here) which will help you remember and use these words from the unit:

argue _____

get ready _____

unless _____

as soon as _____

likely _____

8 Write

a Read this advertisement in a newspaper. The advertisement requests information about four different things. What are they?

b A young man called André wrote a letter to apply for one of the jobs. Read his letter and say which of the four requests for information in the advertisement he <u>doesn't</u> respond to.

Dear Sir or Madam

I am writing to apply for a summer camp job in the UK.

I am an independent and reliable person. [1]<u>Unless I get one of the jobs</u>, I will work hard and I am sure that I will be a good employee.

I think that you need patience and a good sense of humour to work with younger children. I believe I have these qualities, but I also think that [2]<u>they are likely improve</u> through this work. I think I will also learn how to deal with difficult children, and to provide discipline when it is needed.

It has always been my dream to visit Britain. I believe that my English will improve, and I am sure that I [3]<u>will to learn</u> a lot of things about a different and foreign culture.

[4]<u>Thank you for consider</u> my application. I look forward to your reply.

Yours faithfully

André Le Bendit

---

c Each of the <u>underlined</u> phrases 1–4 contains a language mistake. Correct each one.

d Imagine that you want to apply for one of the summer camp jobs. Write your letter in about 120–180 words. (Don't count the opening and your name.)

SUMMER CAMPS UK

Wanted: young people to work on a holiday camp for 10- to 13-year-old children in the UK for a period of three months. Various locations in the country. The work includes organising entertainment for the children and general cleaning duties.

If you are interested in this position, write and tell us:

- why you think you are suitable for the post
- about your level of English (exams you have passed / hope to pass in the future)
- what you think you will gain from working with younger children
- what you think you will gain or learn from being in the UK for three months

Write to PO Box 788, Cheltenham, UK before April 30 this year.

WRITING TIP

Writing a letter for an exam

When you write a letter, especially for a test or an examination, remember that you should always:

- Read the task carefully and do exactly what it asks you to do. In this example, you need to read the advertisement carefully and make sure that you provide all the information that the advertisement asks for. If you miss out important information, you will lose a lot of marks.

- Check your own writing carefully when you have finished. Check for grammar mistakes and for any spelling mistakes. In exams especially, it is easy to make small mistakes under pressure. Give yourself time at the end to check.

- Check your text, if there is a word limit, to make sure that you have used about the required number of words. If you don't write enough words, you will lose marks. If you write far too many, the examiner won't mark much beyond the word limit.

Unit check

1 Fill in the spaces

Complete the text with the words in the box.

until   If   unless   likely   might   probably   for   about   ~~when~~   with

I'm not very sure what to do _____*when*_____ I leave school. [1]_____ I do well in my exams,
I [2]_____ go to university, but I [3]_____ won't get good enough grades – I haven't revised
[4]_____ the exams very much at all. So I think that perhaps I'll get a job, save some money and then
travel a bit, [5]_____ I haven't got any money left. When I told my parents about that, they weren't
very happy and they argued [6]_____ me for a long time. They said they were worried [7]_____ me,
and they didn't want me to go. And I don't think they're [8]_____ to change their minds.
So, [9]_____ I can think of something else, I still won't know what to do when I leave school!   **9**

2 Choose the correct answers

(Circle) the correct answer: a, b or c.

1 _____ the weather's nice this weekend,
   we can have a picnic.
   a (If)   b When   c As soon as

2 Why do you always argue _____ me?
   a to   b at   c with

3 I can't come out tonight – I'm revising
   _____ my exams.
   a for   b about   c to

4 I don't want to leave – I want to stay
   _____ the film finishes.
   a until   b if   c when

5 I'll phone you as soon as I _____ anything.
   a am hearing   b will hear   c hear

6 I can't stand her – she only ever thinks _____ herself.
   a for   b about   c with

7 They won't know _____ you don't tell them.
   a unless   b when   c if

8 Mike's upstairs – he's _____ ready for tonight's party.
   a going   b getting   c being

9 You won't pass the test _____ you study hard.
   a as soon as   b when   c unless   **8**

3 Vocabulary

(Circle) the correct words.

1 What a cool camera! We're going to have
   some fun (with) / for it.

2 I had a great chat by / with my dad last
   night. He's not as old as I thought!

3 If / When you had loads of money, what
   would you do?

4 Let's pray for / with good weather this
   weekend for the party.

5 I dreamed about / by you last night. It was
   a really weird dream.

6 I can't go out tonight. I've got to revise about /
   for my exams.

7 We're in a hurry. We've got to leave until / as soon
   as we've had lunch.

8 It took him hours to get ready for / by the party.
   Was it worth it?

9 I won't help you unless / if you say 'sorry'
   for being mean to me this morning.   **8**

How did you do?

Total: **25**

☺ Very good 20 – 25	☺ OK 14 – 19	☹ Review Unit 4 again 0 – 13

5 Reality TV

1 Grammar

★ *make / let / be allowed to*

a Put the words in the correct order to make sentences.

1 a noise / aren't / to / You / make / allowed
   You aren't allowed to make a noise.

2 travellers / to / The / allowed / enter / weren't / the country
   _____

3 parents / play outside / let / Our / never / us
   _____

4 us / The / didn't / leave / early / let / teacher
   _____

5 mobile / made / switch off / our / They / us / phones
   _____

6 make / Do / before / your parents / bed / you / to / go / 10 o'clock?
   _____

b Look at the signs. Write sentences with *(not) allowed to.*

1 *You aren't allowed to cycle/ride your bike here.*

2 _____

3 _____

4 _____

5 _____

6 _____
   but _____

c Rewrite the sentences. Use the words in brackets.

1 We don't have permission to go into that room. (allow)
   We *aren't allowed to go into that room.*

2 The teacher told us to stay longer at school yesterday. (make)
   The teacher _____ .

3 I don't allow my sister to borrow my things. (let)
   I _____ .

4 My father didn't give me permission to borrow his car. (let)
   My father _____ .

5 You can't smoke here. (allow)
   You _____ .

6 My mum says I have to pay for my own mobile phone. (make)
   My mum _____ .

2 Vocabulary

★ Television

a Match the words with the definitions. Write 1–8 in the boxes.

> 1 episode   2 ~~series~~   3 celebrities   4 viewing figures   5 audience
> 6 sitcoms   7 presenter   8 viewer   9 contestant   10 quiz show

a A group of programmes about the same subject. `2`

b Comedy programmes about the lives of ordinary people. ☐

c A person who takes part in a 10. ☐

d One part of a 2. ☐

e The person who presents a programme. ☐

f People who watch a TV programme in the studio. ☐

g The number of people who watch a programme. ☐

h A programme where people answer questions. ☐

i A person who is watching a TV programme at home (not in the studio). ☐

j Well-known people on television (or in films). ☐

b Complete the sentences with the correct form of the words at the end of each line.

Yesterday evening I watched a ___wonderful___ new quiz show on TV.   WONDER

There are four [1]_____ , who have to answer really hard   CONTEST

questions that the [2]_____ asks them. If they don't know the answer   PRESENT

to a question, they are [3]_____ to phone home and get some help.   ALLOW

And sometimes the [4]_____ at home can phone the programme and   VIEW

ask questions too. The [5]_____ gets a prize of a new car! I think   WIN

it's going to be a very [6]_____ show.   SUCCESS

3 Pronunciation

★ /aʊ/ *allowed*

a ▶CD3 T19 Tick (✔) the words which have the sound /aʊ/ in them. Then listen, check and repeat.

1	how	✔	6	shout	☐
2	know	☐	7	slow	☐
3	now	☐	8	house	☐
4	mouse	☐	9	found	☐
5	loud	☐	10	snow	☐

b ▶CD3 T20 Listen and repeat.

1 How do you know which house it is?

2 I found a mouse in the snow.

3 We heard a loud shout.

4 There was a mouse running loudly round the house.

4 Grammar

★ Modal verbs of obligation, prohibition and permission

a Complete the sentences with the words in the box.

> have to go   mustn't go   can't bring
> don't have to stay   can stay   ~~must bring~~

1 'OK, tomorrow afternoon is sports, so you ___must bring___ your sports clothes, OK?'

2 'Great! My dad says I _____ out as late as I want to.'

3 'Sorry, I'm really late for my meeting. I _____ now.'

4 'Are you bored? Well, look – you _____ here if you don't want to.'

5 'Hey, Alex, that's the girls' toilet, you _____ in there!'

6 'Sorry, you _____ your dog into the library. No animals are allowed in here.'

b Look at the pictures. What are the people saying? Complete the sentences.

1 'We __can't__ leave through here.'

2 'You _____ feed the animals!'

3 'You _____ open it now if you want.'

4 'We _____ show something to prove we're 18.'

5 'I _____ clear up this mess!'

6 'Great! I _____ wear a suit and tie!'

5 Vocabulary

✱ Extreme adjectives and modifiers

a Complete the sentences with the words in the box.

> fantastic enormous awful boiling exhausted
> hilarious ~~tiny~~ starving freezing fascinating

1 A: My dog is so small and cute!
  B: Small? She's __tiny__ !

2 A: Was it hot in Australia?
  B: Yes it was! In fact, it was _____ .

3 A: This is a good song.
  B: Yes, it's _____ .

4 A: Is it cold outside?
  B: It's _____ .

5 A: Is her new flat big?
  B: It certainly is. In fact, it's _____ .

6 A: Are you still feeling bad?
  B: Yes, I feel really _____ .

7 A: He's so funny!
  B: I know. He's _____ .

8 A: What an interesting story!
  B: Yes, it was _____ .

9 A: Are you hungry?
  B: I'm _____ !

10 A: I think they're tired.
  B: Tired? They're _____ !

b **Vocabulary bank** Respond to the questions with *Yes* and an adjective from the word bank. Sometimes more than one answer is possible.

1 The pizza was bad, wasn't it?
  Yes, it was disgusting.

2 Were you scared by that thunder?
  _____

3 Was the band really loud?
  _____

4 Is the soup tasty?
  _____

5 Were you happy with your present?
  _____

6 Are you excited about Disneyland?
  _____

7 Is it really bad news?
  _____

6 Vocabulary

✱ Making new friends

Replace the underlined words with phrasal verbs from the box.

> feel left out   bond with   fit in
> join in

1 Karen's playing with her new puppy. She's trying to make a close connection with it.
  _____

2 What's wrong with you, Sam? Don't you want to be part of the game?
  _____

3 I'm not going out with Harry and his friends any more. I just don't feel like I belong.
  _____

4 Here's a present for you, Tom. I don't want you to think you're not being included.
  _____

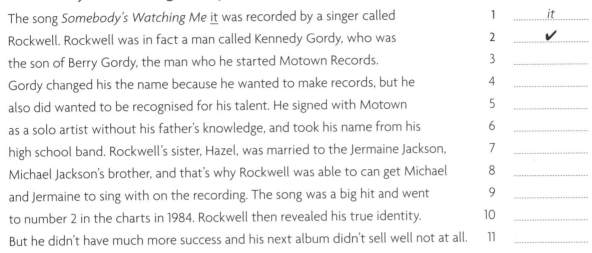

7 Culture in mind

a Read the text about this song. Some of the lines of the text have an extra, unnecessary word. Write the word at the end of the line. If the line is correct, tick it.

Somebody's Watching Me by Rockwell

The song *Somebody's Watching Me* <u>it</u> was recorded by a singer called	1	*it*
Rockwell. Rockwell was in fact a man called Kennedy Gordy, who was	2	✔
the son of Berry Gordy, the man who he started Motown Records.	3	
Gordy changed his the name because he wanted to make records, but he	4	
also did wanted to be recognised for his talent. He signed with Motown	5	
as a solo artist without his father's knowledge, and took his name from his	6	
high school band. Rockwell's sister, Hazel, was married to the Jermaine Jackson,	7	
Michael Jackson's brother, and that's why Rockwell was able to can get Michael	8	
and Jermaine to sing with on the recording. The song was a big hit and went	9	
to number 2 in the charts in 1984. Rockwell then revealed his true identity.	10	
But he didn't have much more success and his next album didn't sell well not at all.	11	

b Read the text again. Mark the statements *T* (true), *F* (false) or *N* (information not given).

1 Rockwell's real name was Berry Gordy. [F]

2 Motown Records started in Detroit, USA. [ ]

3 Berry Gordy knew that his son had signed with Motown. [ ]

4 Jermaine Jackson was Rockwell's brother-in-law. [ ]

5 *Somebody's Watching Me* was a successful single. [ ]

6 Rockwell's next album sold less than ten thousand copies. [ ]

c ▶CD3 T21 Listen to Dave telling a friend about the video for *Somebody's Watching Me*. Put the pictures in the correct order. Write numbers 1–6 in the boxes.

d Here are three lines from the song. Which pictures are they related to?

1 But maybe showers remind me of *Psycho* too much.

2 Well, can the people on TV see me or am I just paranoid?

3 Well, is the mailman watching me?

8 Write

a Paul and Sandra had to write articles for their school magazine. Do not write anything yet, but read what they had to do:

> **Write an article about your favourite television programme. Write about:**
>
> - the kind of programme it is, and how often it is on TV
> - who the people in the programme are
> - what the programme is about
> - what you especially like in the programme and why
> - who you would recommend it to
>
> **Write between 120 and 150 words.**

b Read Paul and Sandra's answers. Complete the sentences with the words from the box.

> been going   very believable
> no matter   ~~on the market~~
> a good reason

c Which of the two articles do you think is better? Why?

d Write an article for your school magazine. Use the same task as Paul and Sandra's.

My favourite programme is *Top Gear*. It's a programme about cars, and I love it because I'm a car freak but also because the presenters are really funny, especially Jeremy Clarkson.

They look at new cars that are [1]*on the market* , and sometimes they're really critical (for example, once Jeremy Clarkson said a car was very cheap, and there was [2]_____ – it was awful!).

There are four presenters – the other three are Richard Hammond, James May and The Stig. It's on once a week, usually at about 8.00 in the evening.   (Paul – 89 words)

My favourite programme is a soap opera on the BBC called *EastEnders*. It's on twice a week, on Tuesday and Thursday evenings, for half an hour each time. It's a story about the lives of people who live in a place called Albert Square, in the east of London. It started in 1985, so the programme's [3]_____ for about twenty years now!

The reason I like *EastEnders* is that the characters are really interesting and you get into their lives. There's a good range of characters, and real things happen to them – illness, divorce, marriage, arguments and so on – so it's [4]_____ . The acting is excellent, too. I think that anyone who enjoys well-written and well-acted soap operas would love *EastEnders*. There's something in it for everyone, [5]_____ how old they are or whether they're a boy or a girl.
(Sandra – 145 words)

WRITING TIP

Organising a writing task

When you are given a writing task, make sure you follow the order of things you are asked to do. This will help you organise your writing.

Look at Paul's article, for example. Here is what he talks about, in this order:

a   the name of the programme
b   what it's about
c   one of the presenters
d   what they do on the programme
e   the presenters (again)
f   when the programme is on

Does Paul write about all the topics he is asked to write about?

Compare Paul's answer to Sandra's. Check:

a   what the task asks for
b   the information Sandra includes in her answer and the order in which she presents it

Unit check

1 Fill in the spaces

Complete the text with the words in the box.

| fun | winner | presenter | contestants | freezing | ~~episodes~~ | had | allowed | made | enormous |

I'll always remember one of the ___episodes___ of *Endurance*, the Japanese game show. There were six
¹_____ , and they were taken to Holland in the middle of winter. They were ²_____ to take
off almost all their clothes and they ³_____ to stand outside in the ⁴_____ weather. Then
the ⁵_____ told them to drink as much water as they possibly could. And they did – they all drank
⁶_____ amounts of water! But that wasn't the competition. When they finished drinking, the
presenter told them that they weren't ⁷_____ to go to the toilet! The ⁸_____ was the
last person to go to the toilet. The presenter made ⁹_____ of them too – it was hilarious!   [9]

2 Choose the correct answers

Circle the correct answer: a, b or c.

1 The _____ in the studio enjoyed the programme
   a lot.
   a viewing   b (audience)   c ratings

2 We don't like wearing a uniform, but the school
   _____ us wear one.
   a makes   b lets   c allowed

3 This soap opera has the highest _____ of any TV
   programme in history!
   a viewers   b viewing figures   c contestants

4 The water in the shower was very cold – in fact,
   it was really _____ !
   a starving   b boiling   c freezing

5 It's a holiday today, so we _____ go to school.
   a don't have to   b must   c have to

6 I watched the first six _____ of the series, but
   then I got bored.
   a ratings   b celebrities   c episodes

7 One day I want to be a _____ in a quiz show
   – I'm sure I'd win!
   a presenter   b viewer   c contestant

8 A few minutes ago, I was hungry – but now
   I'm absolutely _____ !
   a tiny   b starving   c exhausted

9 My school doesn't _____ us to stay inside at
   break time.
   a let   b make   c allow   [8]

3 Vocabulary

Replace the underlined words so that the sentences make sense.

1 That film was absolutely <u>boring</u>. I laughed all
   the way through it. ___*hilarious*___

2 Come over and <u>bond</u> in the fun. _____

3 The forest fire was really <u>terrified</u>.
   _____

4 I'm really <u>excited</u>. I could go to sleep right
   now. _____

5 Your handwriting is so <u>deafening</u>
   I can't read it. _____

6 I don't <u>feel comfortable</u> here. I'm so different from
   everyone else. _____

7 That's a(n) <u>absolutely</u> good idea. _____

8 He presented that wildlife <u>sitcom</u>, but I can't
   remember his name. _____

9 She's an absolutely <u>disgusting</u> singer.
   I think she's my favourite. _____   [8]

How did you do?

Total: [25]

| ☺ Very good 20 – 25 | ☺ OK 14 – 19 | ☹ Review Unit 5 again 0 – 13 |

6 Survival

1 Grammar

✱ Present passive and past passive review

a (Circle) the correct answer: a, b, c or d.

1 Squash is a popular sport that _____ indoors.
   a plays   b (is played)   c played   d was played

2 President John Kennedy _____ in Dallas in November 1963.
   a kills   b is killed   c killed   d was killed

3 Many Japanese people _____ sushi and sashimi.
   a eat   b are eaten   c ate   d were eaten

4 Many animals _____ for scientific experiments in the past.
   a use   b are used   c used   d were used

5 Spanish _____ by a lot of people in the USA.
   a speaks   b is spoken   c spoke   d was spoken

6 Honda is a company that _____ cars.
   a makes   b is made   c made   d was made

b Write sentences using the present simple or past simple passive.

1 The World Trade Centre / destroy / on 11 September 2001
   The World Trade Centre was destroyed on 11 September 2001.

2 A language called Hindi / speak / in many parts of India _____

3 The 2008 Olympic Games / hold / in Beijing _____

4 Boeing 747 planes / call / Jumbos _____

5 Most American films / make / in Hollywood _____

6 The 2006 football World Cup / win / by Italy _____

7 John Lennon / kill / in December 1980 _____

8 The Titanic / sink / by an iceberg _____

9 Gorillas / find / in forests in Africa _____

10 Buildings / design / by architects _____

2 Grammar

✱ Causative *have* (*have something done*)

a Look at the signs. Write sentences about what you can have done at each place.

1 You can _have your pizza delivered._

2 You can have your _____ .

3 You can _____ .

4 You _____ .

5 You _____ .

6 _____ .

① Pizza Home — We deliver pizzas *fast*

② Photo Express — BRING YOUR FILMS HERE — We develop in 30 minutes!

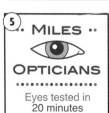
③ Ring & Things — We can pierce your ears in no time at all!

④ Hard and Soft — Let us repair your computer

⑤ MILES OPTICIANS — Eyes tested in 20 minutes

⑥ Clean & Go — We dry-clean clothes in only 12 hours

b ▶CD3 T22 Look at the pictures and write the sentences. Choose words from the box.
Then listen and check.

| photograph | ~~test~~ | computer | repair | car | take | ~~eyes~~ | build | garage | deliver |

1 She *'s having her eyes tested.* 2 They _____ . 3 He _____ .

4 She _____ . 5 They _____ .

3 Pronunciation

✱ Stress pattern in *have something done*

a ▶CD3 T22 Listen again to the sentences in Exercise 2b. Mark the stressed words.

b ▶CD3 T22 Listen again and repeat the sentences.

4 Vocabulary

✱ *make* and *do*

a Match the two parts of the sentences. Write a–h in the boxes.

1 Eat fruit! It'll do [d] a sense to me!

2 I dropped some paint on the floor – it made [ ] b fun of other people.

3 It's not nice to make [ ] c a real mess.

4 You can do it if you make [ ] d you some good.

5 She was very funny but I did [ ] e a lot of money.

6 I don't want to invite Greg. He always makes [ ] f my best not to laugh at her.

7 When he sold his flat he made [ ] g trouble at parties.

8 Why do some people smoke? It doesn't make [ ] h an effort.

b Complete the sentences with the correct form of *make* or *do*.

1 Don't just sit there! _Do_ something!

2 I took the medicine the doctor gave me and it _____ me a lot of good.

3 I've read this page three times – and it still _____ (not) sense to me!

4 I've got a faster computer now, and it _____ a big difference.

5 Yesterday's exam was hard! But I _____ my best.

6 There was a group of boys trying to _____ trouble at the match.

7 I think I _____ a mess of the interview. I didn't know what to say.

8 I'm going to get a job and _____ some money.

Vocabulary bank (Circle) the correct words.

1 We've got to clean the whole house, so let's make a (start) / room right away.

2 I'm interested in the bike you've got for sale. I'd like to make you *a price / an offer*.

3 If you want a sofa in your room, you're going to have to take something out to make *spare / room* for it.

4 Mum, we want to make a *question / request*: can we go for a picnic at the weekend, please?

5 Paul, your father and I need to talk to you. Can you make some *room / time* to sit down with us later today?

6 Sabrina's just got a job as a fashion designer. What a great way to make a *living / job*!

7 Please go back and make *definite / sure* that you locked the front door.

8 The council are planning to knock down some houses to make *way / route* for a new motorway.

5 Grammar

✱ Present perfect passive

a Complete the sentences with the words in the box.

have been killed	has been made
have been sold	have been made
haven't been invited	~~has been built~~

1 A new library ___*has been built*___ in our town.

2 Their new CD only came out last week, but thousands of copies _____ already!

3 There's been an earthquake in our country and a lot of people _____ .

4 Many animals _____ extinct in the last twenty years.

5 They're having a party tomorrow evening – but we _____ !

6 A big effort _____ recently to keep the town clean.

b What has happened in each picture? Complete the sentences with the present perfect passive form of the verbs.

1 The woman ___*has been robbed*___ . (rob)

2 Three houses _____ . (knock down)

3 Their pizzas _____ (not deliver) yet.

4 The bank robbers _____ . (catch)

5 That car _____ (not clean) for weeks!

6 The fire _____ . (put out)

c Rewrite the sentences to make them passive.

1 A man from Liverpool has won the £10-million pound jackpot.

The £10-million pound jackpot was won by a man in Liverpool.

2 Messi scored the winning goal.

The winning goal _____ _____ .

3 A professional decorated our house.

Our house _____ _____ .

4 They didn't deliver our passports to us in time.

Our passports _____ _____ .

5 Mr Brown deals with all complaints.

All complaints _____ _____ .

6 Mary always cut my hair.

I _____ .

6 Grammar

✱ Future passive

a Look at the poster. What will be done if they are elected? Complete the sentences.

1 New schools _will be built_ .
2 Trees and parks _____ .
3 Taxes _____ .
4 Food _____ to poor families.
5 More policemen _____ on the streets.
6 Hospitals _____ .
7 New companies _____ .
8 Pollution _____ .

VOTE FOR US!

We will ...
- build new schools!
- protect trees and parks!
- NOT increase taxes!
- give food to poor families!
- put more policemen on the streets!
- NOT close hospitals!
- help new companies!
- reduce pollution!

b Complete the sentences/questions. Use the future passive form of the verbs.

1 A new swimming pool
will be built (build) in our town next year.

2 It _____ (not finish) until next October.

3 _____ the water _____ (heat)?

4 All the swimmers _____ (supervise) by lifeguards.

5 Children under ten _____ (not allow) to swim without an adult.

6 _____ people who can't swim _____ (give) lessons?

7 Everyday English

a Complete the expressions with the words in the box.

~~mean~~ Any How More all earth

1 I _mean_
2 What on _____ (are you doing)?
3 _____ chance (you could help me)?
4 after _____
5 _____ come (you're late)?
6 _____ or less

b Complete the dialogues with the expressions in Exercise 7a.

1 A: I got the last question wrong.
   B: But it was so easy! _____ you didn't know the answer?

2 A: Like my new coat? It cost me €200!
   B: €200?? That's incredibly expensive! _____ are you doing, buying things like that?

3 A: Have you finished that book?
   B: _____ – I've just got the last ten pages to read.

4 A: Hi, David. What's the matter?
   B: Hi, Mr Jones. The thing is, I missed my bus. _____ you could take me to school?

5 A: You made a complete mess of everything!
   B: Oh, come on. That's not fair. _____ , I did my best.

6 A: He won't lend me his MP4 player! I don't understand why not.
   B: Well, maybe he's using it. And it's his MP4 player, _____ .

8 Listen

▶ CD3 T23 Listen to five short recordings. For each one, (circle) the correct answer: a, b or c.

1 Listen to a teacher who is talking to a group of students about a bus. What time will the bus leave?

   a 8.15

   b 8.30

   c 8.50

2 Listen to a teacher talking to a girl, Sally, about her results. What does the Maths teacher think about Sally's results?

   a She's very happy with Sally's progress.

   b She thinks that Sally could make more progress.

   c She's very angry that Sally hasn't made progress.

3 Mike is talking to Andy. What is different about Andy?

   a He's had his hair cut.

   b He's had his arm tattooed.

   c He's had his ear pierced.

4 A news announcer is talking about an earthquake. How many people have been killed?

   a About four thousand.

   b About four hundred.

   c About fourteen thousand.

5 Listen to a phone conversation – a woman is ordering a pizza. How much will she have to pay for the pizza?

   a £6.25 plus 30p for delivery.

   b £6.25 if she wants the pizza in the next 30 minutes.

   c Nothing if the pizza is not delivered within 30 minutes.

LISTENING TIP

How to answer multiple choice questions

- Read all the choices carefully and make sure you understand them. What do you have to listen for? For example, in number 1 you have to listen for a time.

- Remember that you will need to listen to the whole section before you choose your answer. Never write down the first thing you hear. For example, in number 1, the woman tells the students to be back at the bus at 8.15, but that <u>isn't</u> when the bus will leave. She then goes on to say it will leave 'at half past'. So, what time does the bus leave?

- Remember that you can usually hear the recording twice. Use the second listening either to check your answer, or to help you think about the correct answer.

Unit check

1 Fill in the spaces

Complete the text with the words in the box.

> were   was   have   had   ~~went~~   developed
> made   made   taken   effort

Last year I needed a new passport, so I _____went_____ to a photo shop in town and had my photograph
¹_____ . When I went back two days later to collect the photo, I looked at it and thought it
²_____ awful! The colour was strange, and I was sure it hadn't been ³_____ properly, so I
complained to the man in the shop. I said: 'You've ⁴_____ a mess of this!', but he ⁵_____ fun
of me. The manager asked me if I wanted to ⁶_____ my photo taken again. I wasn't very happy, but
I said OK, sat down and made a big ⁷_____ to smile. This time I ⁸_____ three photos taken,
but when I saw them they ⁹_____ worse than the first one because I looked so angry!   9

2 Choose the correct answers

Circle the correct answer: a, b or c.

1   Work hard and you'll _____ money.

   a do   b (make) c have

2   I need to throw some old clothes away, to make
_____ for the new ones.

   a room   b a mess   c an effort

3   My dad's car broke down, so he had to _____
it repaired.

   a have   b do   c make

4   If you pronounce a language well, it makes a big
_____ for other people.

   a mess   b difference   c progress

5   A prehistoric man _____ last year.

   a was found   b find   c is found

6   She went to the hairdresser's to _____ .

   a cut her hair   b have cut her hair

   c have her hair cut

7   Eating fruit can do you a lot of _____ .

   a best   b good   c better

8   Since last year, a lot of new roads _____ .

   a have been built   b were built   c have built

9   The government says that next year,
taxes will _____ .

   a reduce   b be reduced   c have reduced

8

3 Vocabulary

Complete the dialogue. Write one word in each space.

Pam: Hey, Lucy, have you heard that they want
to knock down the swimming pool to make
_____way_____ for a shopping centre?

Lucy: No way! Well, I think we should all make
a big ¹_____ to stop them! I'm fed up
with the planners making a ²_____ of
our town.

Pam: I agree! I'll do my ³_____ to get
some of our friends involved. Like Gerry.

Lucy: There's no point in asking Gerry. He'll just
make ⁴_____ of what we're trying to
do. He always laughs at us anyway.

Pam: I don't care. We're going to try to
⁵_____ some good in this town. If he
wants to ⁶_____ trouble, or tease us
about it, that's up to him.

Lucy: OK, well first of all let's talk to our parents
and see what ideas they've got.

Pam: Yes, that makes ⁷_____ . They always
have good ideas. So come on – let's make
a ⁸_____ !   8

How did you do?

Total: 25

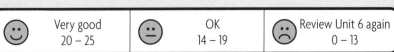

| 😊 Very good 20 – 25 | 😐 OK 14 – 19 | ☹ Review Unit 6 again 0 – 13 |

7 Good and evil

1 Grammar

✱ Gerunds and infinitives

a Find and (circle) seven verbs that are followed by a gerund (→ ←) and seven verbs that are followed by the infinitive. (↓↑)

W	T	R	E	N	J	O	Y	E	E
P	N	O	U	X	G	F	L	P	S
R	A	W	F	I	O	F	O	V	O
O	W	T	S	E	T	E	D	X	O
M	I	N	D	E	E	R	R	J	H
I	M	A	G	I	N	E	O	L	C
S	U	G	G	E	S	T	F	E	H
E	K	I	L	L	E	E	F	A	O
P	S	E	S	I	T	C	A	R	P
O	A	E	V	I	L	O	S	N	E

b Complete the sentences with the gerund or infinitive form of the verbs. Then look at page 55 of the Student's Book to check your answers.

1 Jane can't stand _____living_____ (live) with her evil aunt.

2 Jane later decides _____ (leave) her life teaching at the school.

3 Count Dracula wants _____ (buy) a house near London.

4 Why must the Count avoid _____ (see) him during the day?

5 Some of the younger children imagine _____ (be) chased by a strange beast.

6 Jack promises _____ (kill) the beast.

7 Bilbo Baggins enjoys _____ (live) an ordinary life.

8 Gollum offers _____ (let) him go free if he can solve a riddle.

c Complete the text with the correct form of the verbs in the box.

> write   help   read   ~~smoke~~   help   fight
> kill   play

Everyone knows about Sherlock Holmes, the famous Victorian detective, who enjoyed _____smoking_____ his pipe and practised
[1] _____ his violin while he thought about his latest case. Not so many people are familiar with his enemy, Professor Moriarty.

Whereas Holmes promised [2] _____ evil, Moriarty chose [3] _____ it. In fact, Moriarty offered [4] _____ all the criminals in London.

When Holmes' creator, Sir Arthur Conan Doyle, didn't feel like [5] _____ any more detective stories, he decided [6] _____ both characters. In a famous scene from *The Final Problem* (1893), Moriarty and Holmes fell to their deaths while fighting on top of the Reichenbach waterfalls in Switzerland.

However, under pressure from his readers who missed [7] _____ about their favourite detective, Conan Doyle brought Holmes back to life for 1903's *The Adventure of the Empty House*. So did Moriarty really die? Only one man knows.

d Put the words in the correct order to make sentences.

1 friends / I / really / with / enjoy / time / spending / my

   I really enjoy spending time with my friends.

2 again / see / I / to / you / want / soon

   _____

3 help / school / to / My / offered / me / after / teacher

   _____

4 called / being / detests / Timothy / He

   _____

5 imagine / with / I / getting / angry / can't / him

   _____

6 to / more / to / have / patient / learn / You'll / be

   _____

e Complete the sentences with verbs from box A and box B in the correct forms.

Box A	Box B
feel like miss practise afford avoid mind ~~offer~~ promise	give go speak buy live get up study ~~lend~~

1 Dad ___*offered*___ ___*to lend*___ me his car for the weekend. Where shall we go?

2 I really don't _____ _____ to school today. I want to stay in bed all day!

3 I can't _____ _____ a new computer. I've only saved €300.

4 This city's so noisy. I really _____ _____ by the sea.

5 She _____ _____ me her answer tomorrow. I hope she says 'yes'.

6 I need someone _____ _____ French with. I've got my oral test next week.

7 I don't _____ _____ early but I prefer to sleep in at weekends.

8 I always _____ _____ the night before a test.

2 Vocabulary

✱ Noun suffixes

a Write the noun forms of the words in the box in the correct columns.

> kind   popular   ~~relax~~   protect   prefer   probable   react
> enjoy   prepare   imagine   agree   differ   entertain   possible

-ation	-ence	-ment	-ness	-ion	-ity
relaxation					

b Complete the text with the correct form of the words.

James Bond's [1] ___*popularity*___ is as big as it has ever been. Today's audiences continue to [2] _____ 007, half a century after his first appearance in 1962's *Dr No*.
Bond still offers the world [3] _____ from villains by using his [4] _____ .
Young or old, male or female, audiences all [5] _____ that Bond films are still great [6] _____ .

POPULAR
ENJOYMENT

PROTECT
IMAGINE
AGREEMENT
ENTERTAIN

c **Vocabulary bank** Complete the sentences with the correct form of the words.

1 I love films with lots of _____action_____ . (act)

2 That's a bad cut. I think you might need hospital _____ . (treat)

3 I wonder what kind of _____ we'll get this time. (punish)

4 What a great _____ ! Let's go right now. (suggest)

5 Will I get an _____ to your party? (invite)

6 Looking directly at the sun can cause _____ . (blind)

7 You need a lot of _____ to write a good sitcom. (create)

8 Let me show you this great job _____ . (advertise)

9 It's _____ to think you can pass the exams without studying. (mad)

3 Pronunciation

* Word stress

a ▶ CD3 T24 Listen and <u>underline</u> the stressed syllables. In which pairs of words does the stress change?

1 prep<u>are</u>   prepar<u>a</u>tion   3 enjoy   enjoyment   5 protect   protection

2 prefer   preference   4 lazy   laziness   6 popular   popularity

b Practise saying each pair of words.

4 Grammar

* Verbs with gerunds or infinitives

a Match the sentences with the pictures. Write A–D in the boxes.

1 I stopped to have a look at the map. | B |

2 I remember posting the letter. | |

3 I remembered to post the letter. | |

4 I stopped looking at the map. | |

b Match the questions and the answers.

1 Did you remember to phone Jane?

2 Don't you remember telling that joke before?

3 Why are you so late?

4 Do you want a hamburger?

5 When are you going to stop playing that game?

a No thanks, I've stopped eating meat.

b I'm on the last level. Nearly done!

c No, I'll give her a call now.

d I stopped to buy you some flowers.

e Oh, I'm sorry. Well, it's still funny.

c Circle the correct words. Sometimes there is more than one possibility.

1 It's started to snow / snowing. Snowball fights!

2 I remember to see / seeing that girl at Rachel's party. Who is she?

3 I hate to watch / watching romantic films.

4 I stopped to eat / eating chicken years ago.

5 I stopped to buy / buying a CD on my way home.

6 She loves to go / going to the cinema on Saturday afternoons.

7 Did you remember to tell / telling Owen where we're meeting tonight?

8 They began to work / working on the road at 6am. Can you believe it?

5 Fiction in mind

a Read more from *Water of Wanting* by Frank Brennan. What happened to the two sets of laboratory mice? What do you think the water contains?

Jean Pascal put a small drop of clear liquid into the drinking water of his mice.

[1] .... But Jean soon noticed that when there was liquid in the water, they came back to drink it more than usual. They couldn't have been thirsty any more, but they drank. He needed to check this carefully.

Jean was now a brilliant chemist. He worked in Montreal, Canada, for a large chemical company. His company made a lot of different chemicals – including chemicals for food, which are often called additives. Additives give food a different colour or flavour or even make it last longer.

[2] ....

The mice kept coming back for more water. Their stomachs were already completely full of liquid, but they still wanted to drink more. They just couldn't get enough water which had Jean's additive in it. They didn't want to eat any food at all. [3] .... And, amazingly, they were still trying to reach the water when they died.

He cut the amount of WOW that he added to his mice's water by half. [4] ....Then he added much smaller amounts of WOW: the mice drank less, but they still came back for little drinks of water all the time. These little drinks were still far more than the mice needed. It was as if they had become addicted to water. They weren't interested in anything else. They didn't even want food. This time they didn't die of too much water. They all died of hunger.

(from Brennan, F. (2009) 'Water of Wanting' in *Tasty Tales*, CUP: pp 4–6)

b Read the extract again and put one of the following sentences in each space. There is one sentence you won't need.

A Food companies pay a lot of money for additives which work well.

B Normally, the mice drank only when they were thirsty.

C Soon they died because their tiny bodies were too full of water.

E It was big and expensive and it exploded in his face.

F The results were the same.

c Choose the correct way to complete the statements, according to the text.

1 In his first experiment, Jean observed that
   a the mice were eating more than usual.
   b the liquid affected the mice's thirst.
   c the mice died almost immediately.
   d he had put too much liquid into the water.

2 Food additives
   a can keep food fresh for longer.
   b are mostly manufactured in Canada.
   c are natural parts of most food.
   d do not change the way something tastes.

3 The first group of mice
   a drank all the water at once.
   b finally became satisfied and stopped drinking.
   c ate too much and couldn't drink any more water.
   d didn't realise the water was killing them.

4 In the second experiment,
   a the WOW concentration was doubled.
   b the mice still drank more than was necessary.
   c the mice drank even more than before.
   d the mice died the same way as in the first experiment.

Skills in mind

6 Listen

a ▶ **CD3 T25** You will hear part of an interview with a film critic about how monsters have changed in films. Listen and tick (✔) the characters he mentions.

Friday 13th: Jason

Frankenstein: Frankenstein's Monster

Dracula

Nightmare on Elm Street: Freddie

b ▶ **CD3 T25** Listen again and complete the sentences.

1 People have always been fascinated by monsters and the dark side ....

2 Without evil there is no such thing ....

3 The late .... and early part of the .... was the golden age of the monster.

4 Frankenstein's Monster and Mr Hyde were the results of humans trying to ....

5 .... have no motivation. They're very two-dimensional.

6 Freddie, Jason and Michael Myers are really just three ....

7 Audiences just want to see how many ....

8 All these monsters do is make us scared to go to ....

LISTENING TIP

How to complete sentences

- As with all listening exercises, read through the questions carefully before you listen. This will help prepare you for what you might expect to hear.

- Try to predict what the missing word(s) might be. However, remember that your predictions may be wrong, so you still need to listen carefully to check.

- You will not always hear the exact words that are in the question. Listen carefully for different words that are used that have the same meaning.

  For example, question 1 says:

  People have always been fascinated by monsters.

  You heard:

  The human race has always been extremely interested in monsters.

- You are only expected to write between one and three words. No more.

- Finally, read through your answers carefully. Make sure they are grammatically correct and check your spelling.

Unit check

1 Fill in the spaces

Complete the text with the words in the box.

> getting   to get   to play   imagination
> characters   strategy   ~~entertainment~~
> graphics   playing   popularity

The best form of __entertainment__ for me is a good computer game. One with cool ¹_____ that seem like real people. And it has to have good ²_____ , so that you feel like you're right there in the action. I don't like games that are too simple. I like trying to work out the ³_____ of the game – you know, I enjoy ⁴_____ into the mind of the game's creator. The best games need a lot of ⁵_____ , because there are so many boring games out there. The ⁶_____ of a game doesn't really matter to me – just because everyone wants ⁷_____ it doesn't mean it's good. I actually don't mind ⁸_____ older games. I'd love ⁹_____ the original PacMan one day – it's amazing.

| 9 |

2 Choose the correct answers

Circle the correct answer: a, b or c.

1 Stephen Spielberg's got such a fantastic _____ .
   a imagine   b imaginity   c (imagination)

2 I must remember _____ the DVD back to the shop today.
   a taking   b to take   c take

3 I like a computer game that _____ me, and makes me think.
   a challenges   b strategies   c controls

4 That teacher is well known for her _____ .
   a kind   b kindly   c kindness

5 You should _____ drinking too many fizzy drinks. They're not good for you.
   a choose   b avoid   c afford

6 They don't feel like _____ to the party tonight.
   a going   b to going   c to go

7 My parents don't _____ about anything.
   a agree   b agreement   c agreeing

8 After walking six kilometres, they stopped _____ a drink and a rest.
   a to have   b having   c have

9 I suggested _____ a cheaper phone, but he didn't listen.
   a buy   b you to buy   c buying

| 8 |

3 Vocabulary

Complete the sentences with nouns made from the underlined words.

1 He thinks it's possible, but I don't see any __possibility__ of it happening.

2 Are they different? I can't see any _____ between them.

3 So what if he's popular! I don't care about _____ .

4 Did you say you want me to protect you? Why do you need _____ ?

5 You're so creative! I wish I had your _____ .

6 Please don't punish me. I can't stand _____ .

7 A: Did you enjoy the game?
   B: It wasn't what I'd call _____ .

8 I've been preparing for this all week. That's enough _____ .

9 She reacted badly. In fact, I was really surprised at her _____ .

| 8 |

How did you do?

Total: | 25 |

| 😊 | Very good 20 – 25 | 😐 | OK 14 – 19 | 🙁 | Review Unit 7 again 0 – 13 |

8 Be honest!

1 Grammar

✱ Second conditional review

a Match the sentences with the pictures. Write 1–6 in the boxes.

1 If we win the World Cup, it will be the best day of my life.

2 If I had my shorts, I would play football.

3 If the rain doesn't stop tomorrow, we won't be able to have a barbecue.

4 If it rained tomorrow, I would be very happy.

5 If you are eighteen, you can come in.

6 If you were eighteen, you could come in.

b Complete the text. Use the correct form of the verbs and *would*, *'d*, *wouldn't* or *might*.

Imagine I ____*found*____ (find) €100 in the street. I'm not sure what I [1] ____*'d do*____ (do). If I [2] _____ (take) it to the police station, they [3] _____ (not be) interested. If I [4] _____ (ask) in the nearest shop, the assistant [5] _____ (say) it was hers. If I [6] _____ (give) it to a homeless person, they [7] _____ (spend) it on beer. If I [8] _____ (tell) my friends, they [9] _____ (want) to spend it and if I [10] _____ (keep) it, I [11] _____ (feel) guilty. I hope I never find €100 in the street!

c Put the words in order to make the sentences.

1 your / go / asked / friend / Say / you / best / shoplifting / to

   Say your best friend asked you to go shoplifting.

2 you / fighting / the / saw / Imagine / two / street / men / in

   _____

3 forgot / really / test / Suppose / to / for / revise / a / you / important

   _____

4 in / found / you / cinema / Say / €500 / the

   _____

5 if / borrowed / friend's / and / it / you / What / broke / your / stereo ?

   _____

d Write your own answers to the questions in Exercise 1c. What would you do?

1 *I'd tell him I thought it was wrong.*

2 _____

_____

3 _____

_____

4 _____

_____

5 _____

_____

2 Vocabulary

⭐ Crimes

a Read the descriptions of the crimes and write the names of the crimes in the spaces. Choose from the words in the box.

> burglary joyriding arson
> shoplifting pick-pocketing
> ~~vandalism~~

1 'Have you seen the church? They've sprayed graffiti all over it.' ___*vandalism*___

2 'They broke a window to get in but they only took the TV and the DVD player.' _____

3 'When he was only twelve, he broke into a car and drove it around, just for fun.'

_____

4 'I was on the bus. I felt a hand and when I looked for my wallet it was gone.' _____

5 'The police are treating the fire at the school as suspicious.'

_____

6 'Excuse me, could I take a look in your bag?' _____

⭐ Crime verbs

b Complete the sentences with the words in the box.

> caught wrong into law ~~away~~ crime

1 Sixteen-year-old John's been getting ___*away*___ with shoplifting for two years; until last week when he got _____ with ten CDs hidden in his coat.

2 When Steve was a teenager he was always getting _____ trouble with the police for vandalism, shoplifting and things like that. Now he's 25 and he's committed a more serious _____ – arson. He burned the town library down.

3 Helen knew she was doing something _____ . She knew that going at 140 kph was breaking the _____ but she didn't think she would have an accident. She's OK but four innocent people are in hospital with serious injuries.

c What punishment do you think each of the people in Exercise 2b should get? Choose from the words in the box.

> pay a fine   be put on probation
> do community service   be sent to prison

1 *John should do 30 hours community service and be put on probation.*

2 _____

3 _____

d **Vocabulary bank** Match the words 1–8 with their definitions. Write a–h in the boxes.

1 murderer [c]   a a person who attacks someone in the street and takes their valuables
2 assassin [ ]   b the act of killing another person
3 mugger [ ]   c a person who kills another person or people
4 break-in [ ]   d someone who steals things
5 murder [ ]   e the act of taking things that do not belong to you
6 mug [ ]   f the act of entering someone's house illegally, usually by breaking a window
7 thief [ ]   g someone who deliberately kills a well-known person
8 theft [ ]   h to attack someone and take things from them

3 Grammar

✱ *I wish / if only*

a ⟨Circle⟩ the correct words.

1 I wish I *am* / ⟨*was*⟩ a bit thinner.
2 If only I *could* / *can* go to the party tonight.
3 My sister wishes she *has* / *had* a boyfriend.
4 Darren wishes he *didn't* / *doesn't* spend so much time playing computer games.

5 My dad wishes he *wasn't* / *isn't* so busy.
6 If only she *loves* / *loved* me.
7 I wish I *don't* / *didn't* have so much homework.
8 If only I *know* / *knew* the answer.

b Mike isn't happy. Read what he says and write *I wish / if only* sentences.

1 'I can't drive and I don't have a car.'

   He wishes he could drive and he wishes
   he had a car.

2 'My parents don't understand me.'

   ----

3 'My little brother annoys me all the time.'

   ----

4 'My computer's broken.'

   ----

5 'I don't have enough money to buy a new bike.'

   ----

6 'I can't find my house keys.'

   ----

7 'I'm too shy to talk to girls.'

   ----

c Look at the pictures and write *I wish / if only* sentences for each of the people.

1 *If only I wasn't so hungry.*   2 _____   3 _____

4 _____   5 _____   6 _____

7 _____   8 _____   9 _____

4 Pronunciation

✱ *I wish ...* and *if only ...*

▶ **CD3 T26** Listen and repeat. Pay attention to the stress of *if only* and *I wish*.

1 I wish I was somewhere else.
2 If only he loved me.
3 I wish I didn't have so many problems.

4 If only I could go to the party.
5 I wish it was Saturday.
6 If only she understood.

5 Listen

Use the words from the song *I wish* to complete the sentences. Check with the song on page 64 of the Student's Book.

> scene   hang around   ~~freeze~~   twist   breeze   turn into

1 You'll _____*freeze*_____ if you go out without a coat. It's snowing.

2 It was a perfect day on the beach. There was a nice hot sun with a gentle _____ to keep you cool.

3 There was this really scary scene in the film – the man started to _____ and turn until he _____ this terrible monster, half man and half wolf.

4 My grandad was part of the music _____ in Liverpool in the 1960s. He says he used to _____ with The Beatles, but I'm not sure if I believe that.

6 Study help

✱ Key word transformations

In this type of exercise you have to rewrite a sentence using a given word so that it means the same. For example:

John is interested in knowing more about astronomy. LIKE

John _____ know more about astronomy.

- Think carefully about the key word. How does this relate to the sentence? For example, *is interested in* can have a similar meaning to *would like*.

- Is the key word part of a phrasal verb? Is it part of a fixed expression?

- Identify and <u>underline</u> the part of the sentence you need to change. For example, *is interested in knowing*.

- What else do you need to know about the key word? For example, *would like* is followed by the infinitive.

- Think carefully about the tense. Usually both sentences will be in the same tense, but be careful with words like *wish* and conditionals, when the tense may change.

- Always check your answer carefully for basic mistakes.

7 Write

a Read the composition and put the paragraphs in the correct order. Write 1–4 in the boxes.

'There would be less crime on the streets if the minimum age for prison was lowered to 16.' Discuss this statement and give your own opinion.

A If the minimum age for prison was lowered to 16, we would probably see an immediate drop in crime for two reasons. Firstly, many potential teenage criminals might think twice before getting involved if they knew they could go to prison. Secondly, those who continued to commit crimes but got caught would be in prison and unable to cause more trouble. ☐

B I believe the answer to helping solve the problem of teenage crime is in education. Teenage criminals need to be shown that crime does not pay and taught other ways to live. ☐

C Unfortunately, the benefits of such a harsh new law would be temporary. In prison, these teenagers would meet much more experienced criminals and learn new ways to get away with crimes. When they left prison a few years later, the majority of them would be much more dangerous than when they went in. Crime on the street would soon increase again. ☐

D A survey in the UK shows that about 50% of children between the ages of 11 and 17 have broken the law. However, the most serious statistics are those about boys aged 15 to 16 who are involved in serious crimes such as burglary, physical violence and vandalism. ☐

b Match the paragraphs with the summaries 1–4. Write A–D in the boxes.

1 Arguments that agree with the title ☐

2 An introduction ☐

3 The writer's opinion ☐

4 Arguments that disagree with the title ☐

WRITING TIP

Developing a discursive composition (1)

- A useful way to organise discursive compositions is in four paragraphs:

  1 introduction
  2 arguments for or against
  3 arguments against or for
  4 your opinion

- Read the title carefully and decide what your opinion is. Make notes to support your argument.

- Make notes under two headings: *for* and *against*. Use these for your second and third paragraphs.

- Good ways to start a composition are:
  – Statistics: 'A survey in the UK shows that about 50% of children ...'
  – A question to be answered: 'Why is society so worried about crime?'
  – A statement supporting the title: 'We live in a violent society ...'

c Write a composition of about 250 words about this statement:

'The world would be a better place if people under 40 made the decisions.' Discuss.

Unit check

1 Fill in the spaces

Complete the text with the words in the box.

would	imagine	caught	down	put
away	can	~~wish~~	could	into

You have an important composition for your History lesson in the morning. It's 10 pm. You _____wish_____
you had started earlier and it's really beginning to get you ¹_____. Well, ²_____ you
³_____ pay ten Euros to have it done for you and get an A grade. What ⁴_____ you do?
Cheating via the internet is a serious problem for many schools and universities, and many students
are getting ⁵_____ with it. For a small price, students ⁶_____ buy work from one of many
websites. However, if a student gets ⁷_____, they can get ⁸_____ serious trouble.
Most schools will ⁹_____ the student on probation; many will even expel them.

9

2 Choose the correct answers

Circle the correct answer: a, b or c.

1 He _____ the job down because the money
   wasn't very good.
   a talked b played c turned

2 If I _____ your help, I would ask you for it.
   a needed b need c will need

3 Nobody saw us. I think we've got _____ with it.
   a away b over c up

4 My car's _____ down three times this month.
   a gone b broken c run

5 My little brother's always _____ into trouble
   with my parents.
   a being b going c getting

6 He didn't slow _____ although the road
   was wet.
   a down b up c over

7 They made him _____ 100 hours of community
   service for vandalising the old factory.
   a spend b make c do

8 If only I _____ have so many problems.
   a didn't b don't c not

9 You might go to prison if you _____ the law.
   a do b make c break

8

3 Vocabulary

Use the words in brackets to form a word
that fits in the gap.

These days more young people are
¹____breaking____ (BREAK) the law than ever
– there are more adolescent ²_____
(CRIME) than ever before. But it isn't all bad
news. On the whole, young people aren't
³_____ (COMMIT) what are considered
serious crimes – like murder – but they often
do things like going into some stores and
⁴_____ (SHOP) – i.e. taking goods without
paying. Another more common crime for young
people is to steal cars. They take the cars and go
⁵_____ (RIDE). It often ends in disaster as
they frequently end up crashing the cars. Sadly,
many young people are found guilty of
⁶_____ (VANDAL), and they often can't
even explain why they did the damage in the
first place. Luckily, there are not too many young
⁷_____ (ARSON), which is a good thing.
But for young criminals, there is no point
⁸_____ (SEND) them to prison. One of
the better options is to give them some hours
of ⁹_____ (COMMUNE) service. That way
they pay back the people they live with.

8

How did you do?

Total: **25**

😊	Very good 20 – 25	😐	OK 14 – 19	🙁	Review Unit 8 again 0 – 13

1 Grammar

✳ Linkers of contrast: *however / although / despite / even though / in spite of*

a Complete the sentences with the words in the box.

> didn't go   didn't buy   bought   ~~went~~   don't feel like   feel like

1 Although I wasn't feeling very well, I __went__ to school.

2 Despite the fact it was expensive, I _____ it.

3 Even though it's my birthday, I _____ celebrating.

4 In spite of the fact the sun was shining, we _____ for a picnic.

5 I know it's only 9 pm. However, I _____ going to bed.

6 Even though they're my favourite band, I _____ their new CD.

b Look at the pictures. (Circle) the correct words.

1 The place looks beautiful. *In spite of /* (*However,*) I couldn't live there.

2 *Although / Despite* I usually love horror films, *The Blair Witch Project* was too scary for me.

3 So you haven't done any work, *even though / in spite of* your exams start tomorrow?

4 *Although / However* I can't speak English very well, I can understand American films fine.

5 We had a fantastic holiday *although / in spite of* the rain.

c Rewrite the sentences. Use the words in brackets.

1 Although she doesn't like rock music, she went to the concert. (despite)

   She went to the concert, despite the fact that she doesn't like rock music.

2 We could understand him, even though his accent was very strong. (in spite of)

   _____

   _____

3 Despite not being very hungry, I ate two pieces of cake. (although)

   _____

   _____

4 The main course was delicious, but the dessert was a bit disappointing. (however)

   _____

   _____

5 Even though he's not very tall, he plays basketball really well. (despite)

   _____

   _____

2 Pronunciation

✳ /əʊ/ *though*

▶ **CD3 T27** Listen and repeat. Pay attention to the sound /əʊ/.

1 Nobody knows except Joe.
2 Don't drive so slowly in the snow.
3 Even though she didn't go, I enjoyed the show.
4 Although she won't tell me, I already know.

3 Vocabulary

✳ Problems

a Complete the sentences with the prepositions in the box.

> up   away   over   on   up   out
> over   ~~up~~   back

1 I'll be home late tonight. A problem's *come __up__ at* work.

2 If you've got a problem at school, why don't you *talk it* _____ with your teacher?

3 I can't *make* _____ *my mind* about what to wear tonight.

4 Don't worry about it. I'm sure it'll *go* _____ by itself.

5 I can't give you a decision now. Can I have a few minutes to *think it* _____ ?

6 When nobody knows what to do, Dan always *comes* _____ *with* a great idea.

7 Why don't you *sleep* _____ *it* and give me an answer tomorrow?

8 That's a good point but I'd like to *come* _____ to it a bit later.

9 Let's try to *sort* _____ who is doing what before we start.

b Complete the text with the correct form of the expressions in *italics* in Exercise 3a.

The problem ___*came up*___ (appeared) really unexpectedly. It was a simple question but I couldn't ¹_____ (suggest) an answer.

I wanted some time to ²_____ (keep it in my mind) but I had to ³_____ (decide) quickly. It wasn't the sort of problem you needed to ⁴_____ (take more time) and there were people waiting behind me.

Maybe I could ⁵_____ (discuss it) with the assistant? No, she didn't look very interested.

This was one problem that wasn't going to ⁶_____ (disappear) by itself. And I couldn't ⁷_____ (return) to it later. I had to ⁸_____ (find a solution) now. And then she asked me again, 'Would you like French fries or onion rings with your hamburger?'

c **Vocabulary bank** (Circle) the correct words.

1 We need some good advice on how to (deal with)/ *share* this problem.

2 Will it *cause / invent* a problem if I leave the lesson early today?

3 Let's hope we can do this without *walking / running* into too many problems.

4 Deciding on the best way to start my presentation tomorrow is turning into a real *headache / drawback*.

5 My young brother's teachers say that he's behaving like a *potential / problem* child these days.

6 Thanks for your help. It's true what they say – a problem shared really is a problem *halved / cut*.

7 Let's try and *jump / overcome* the problem together.

8 The trip sounds great but not having a car will be a *solution / drawback*.

4 Grammar

✷ Modal verbs of deduction (present)

a Match the two parts of the sentences. Write a–f in the boxes.

1 He can't be hungry,	[d]	a she's his best friend!
2 He must be hungry,	[ ]	b he didn't have a very big lunch.
3 He might be hungry,	[ ]	c he doesn't have a phone!
4 She must know his phone number,	[ ]	d he's just eaten two large pizzas!
5 She can't know his phone number,	[ ]	e she's a friend of his sister's.
6 She might know his phone number,	[ ]	f he hasn't eaten for 48 hours!

b Rewrite the sentences so they mean the opposite.

1 It might not be true.
   It might be true. _____

2 She must be happy.
   _____

3 They might speak English.
   _____

4 You can't like olives!
   _____

5 They might not know.
   _____

6 He must live near here.
   _____

c Complete the sentences with *must*, *can't* or *might*.

1 That plate's just come out of the oven. It
   ___must___ be hot.

2 They're speaking Spanish, and I think they're from
   South America. They _____ be from Peru.

3 She _____ know. It's a secret!

4 I'm not sure what it is. It _____ be some
   kind of monkey.

5 Everyone passes that exam. It _____ be
   very difficult.

6 That bird's eating the bananas. It _____
   like them!

d Write sentences about the pictures. Use *can't* and *must*.

1 Her boyfriend sends her
   flowers every day.
   He must love her a lot.

2 They've been walking for two
   days. They _____
   _____ .

3 Hardly anyone came to see
   them. They _____
   _____ .

4 They nearly fell asleep. It
   _____ .

5 There were cameras
   everywhere. She _____ .

6 He spent another birthday on
   his own. He _____ .

New Animals

In northern Vietnam, in thick forests in the North Annamite Mountains, there is a wildlife park called Vu Quang. In 1986, the area was made an official forest reserve. In 2002, 550 square kilometres of the area were declared a National Park. Vu Quang is no ordinary park, though. It's in an area that is hard to get to, for one thing. And it's an area that's difficult to walk through because the rocks are covered with algae and are very slippery. But that's not all that is unusual about Vu Quang. In the last twenty years, several new species of animals that have never been seen anywhere in the world before have been discovered there. Some of them are so new that scientists haven't given them official names yet!

The new animals discovered at the park include the Vu Quang ox or Saola, a 'slow' deer, a giant muntjac (the world's largest, in fact), a black deer and a 'holy' goat. Five new species of fish have also been found there, as well as two species of amphibians and 15 species of reptiles.

The Saola was the first new species of large mammal to be discovered in more than fifty years, so it caused a lot of excitement in the scientific world. It is a strange goat-like creature that looks as if it is somehow related to cattle. It has horns that can be between one and two feet long, and that seem to come out of the animal's head at slightly different angles. That's where the animal got its name from: 'Saola' in Vietnamese means 'spinning wheel posts'.

The creature had hidden safely for generations in the Vu Quang area. But once it was discovered, it was in danger. Hunters have no respect for new species. Sadly, the Saola is now being hunted and may well end up as another endangered species.

a Choose the correct answer: a, b, c or d.

1 Between 1986 and 2002, the area was
   a a national park.
   b a mountain.
   c a wildlife reserve.
   (d) a forest reserve.

2 It wouldn't be a good idea to go trekking in the area because
   a there are too many rocks.
   b it's cold and wet.
   c it's slippery underfoot.
   d it's easy to get lost.

3 Some of the new species
   a don't have official names.
   b are birds.
   c have been seen elsewhere in the world.
   d were discovered elsewhere first.

4 The largest _____ in the world has been discovered at Vu Quang.
   a goat
   b muntiac
   c ox
   d deer

5 The Saola is so named because it
   a looks like a goat.
   b has a strange head.
   c is related to cattle.
   d has weird horns.

6 The Saola and other new species are now
   a being hunted.
   b increasing in numbers.
   c hidden from view.
   d endangered.

b Match the words 1–6 with their definitions. Write a–f in the boxes.

1 official — [d]
2 algae
3 slippery
4 angle
5 generation
6 respect

a green plants that grow on rocks in water
b the shape made when two lines meet
c admiration and appreciation
d connected with authority
e causing things to slip and slide because it is wet
f period of time between people being born and having their own offspring

6 Read

Read the film review of *Conspiracy Theory* and choose from the list (A–G) the phrase which best summarises each part (1–6) of the article. There is one extra phrase you won't need.

A   Mad Mel

B   A disappointing ending

C   The man who knows too much

D   The perfect couple

E   A reluctant heroine

F   A villain to remember

G   An exciting love story

READING TIP

Matching summaries with paragraphs

- First of all, do not look at the summary phrases to start with. Read the text completely first.

- Think of your own short summary of each part of the text.

- Now read the summary phrases. Do any match your own summaries? Write in the answers.

- Look at the remaining summary phrases carefully. Try and match vocabulary in them to vocabulary in the passage.

- Finally, never leave an answer space empty. If you really have no idea, try to guess.

1

Mel Gibson is Jerry Fletcher, a New York taxi driver with a conspiracy theory for everything. He publishes his ideas on the internet. One day one of his theories upsets some very powerful men and suddenly his life is in serious danger.

2

The only person who can help him is also the woman he is secretly in love with. Julia Roberts plays Alice Sutton, a justice department lawyer. She wants nothing to do with Fletcher at first but suddenly finds herself drawn into his world.

3

Conspiracy Theory is a well-written, entertaining film, which successfully mixes two popular genres. As a thriller, there is plenty of action to keep the audience on the edge of their seats and, as a romance, we end up believing that a top lawyer really could fall in love with a taxi driver.

4

Perhaps the reason for this is in the strength of the acting. Gibson is at his best as the paranoid Fletcher (so paranoid that he keeps his food locked in canisters, locked inside his fridge).

And Julia Roberts reminds us that as well as being one of the most beautiful women on the planet, she is also one of the world's finest actresses.

5

But good as Gibson and Roberts are, the best performance of the film is from *Star Trek's* Patrick Stewart as Dr Jones, a psychologist from a sinister government department. Every minute he is on the screen he leaves the audience wondering what evil he will do next.

6

My only criticism is about the last twenty minutes of the film, when director Richard Donner forgets his convincing, tense storyline and the film descends into a traditional good vs. bad shoot-out. Maybe because he's working with Mel Gibson again, Donner suddenly seems to think he's directing the next in his series of *Lethal Weapon* movies.

Unit check

1 Fill in the spaces

Complete the text with the words in the box.

| result | came up | go away | minds | official | ~~conspiracy~~ | Although | coming back | Moreover | ignored |

From the death of Lady Diana to the UFO crash at Roswell, everybody loves a good __conspiracy__ theory.
[1]_____ most of us forget them quickly, there are some people who dedicate their lives to them.
As a [2]_____ there are now hundreds of web pages on the subject. [3]_____ , books and films
about them are released every year.
Some conspiracy theories won't [4]_____ – they just keep [5]_____ . A survey done in 2003
to mark the 40th anniversary of JFK's death [6]_____ with the amazing statistic that 74% of Americans
don't believe the [7]_____ story. American people have made up their [8]_____ and JFK
is one conspiracy that refuses to be [9]_____ .

9

2 Choose the correct answers

(Circle) the correct answer: a, b or c.

1 Although _____ the nightclub, I don't want
to go there again.
   a I liking   b liking   c (I liked)

2 Should I buy the red dress or blue one? I can't
_____ my mind up.
   a make   b decide   c do

3 It's not so serious. I'm sure we can _____ it out.
   a make   b sort   c think

4 I decided to travel by train, _____ it was more
expensive than the bus.
   a despite   b even though   c however

5 It's boiling today. It _____ be 35°C at least.
   a might   b must   c can't

6 I've got a problem and I want to _____ it
over with you.
   a say   b talk   c speak

7 _____ knowing a lot about computers, she
couldn't solve the problem.
   a Despite   b However   c Although

8 Why don't you _____ on it and make a
decision in the morning?
   a sleep   b relax   c lie

9 She didn't go to my party. She _____ like me
very much.
   a can't   b must   c might

8

3 Vocabulary

Complete the text. Write one word in each space.

I was working on my go-kart the other day when I _____ran_____ into a few problems. I wasn't sure how
to [1]_____ with them, but Dad said he would help and that we would be able to [2]_____ it
out. He sat down for a few minutes to [3]_____ it all over, then he [4]_____ up with an answer.
'I know what's [5]_____ the problem,' he said. 'And I'm sure we can [6]_____ it together!'
And sure enough, after fifteen minutes my go-kart was working again. My dad's like that. When he
[7]_____ up his mind to do something, he does it! Of course I said thanks for his help: Dad just
said 'That's OK – a problem shared is a problem [8]_____ !'

8

How did you do?

Total: 25

| ☺ Very good 20 – 25 | ☺ OK 14 – 19 | ☹ Review Unit 9 again 0 – 13 |

10 Mysterious places

1 Grammar
✱ Modals of deduction (past)

a Circle the correct words.

1 She must have left because her car is *still here / (not here.)*
2 They can't have played well because they *lost / won.*
3 He must have lost my number because he *phoned / didn't phone* me.
4 You can't have seen my brother because I *have / haven't got* any brothers!
5 We must have done something wrong because he looks really *angry / happy.*
6 I can't have eaten your ham sandwich because I *eat / don't eat* meat.

b Complete the dialogue about the objects in the photo with the words in the box.

> can't have built   might be   could have built   must weigh   could have been
> don't believe   must have been   ~~might have used~~

Sally: Wow, look at them. They're amazing. What do you think they were used for?

Mike: The guidebook says that nobody's sure, but the people here *might have used* them to honour important people on the island.

Sally: I think they ¹ _____ images of gods that the island people worshipped.

Mike: You ² _____ right.

Sally: Do you think that aliens ³ _____ them?

Mike: No, I ⁴ _____ that.

Sally: But humans ⁵ _____ them. Each statue ⁶ _____ hundreds of kilograms.

Mike: But they did build them. Our ancestors ⁷ _____ more intelligent than we think!

c Complete the sentences with *must, can't* or *might/could* and the verb.

1 The exam *must have been* (be) very difficult. Only one person passed.
2 He _____ (leave) the country. He hasn't got a passport.
3 Our dog didn't come home last night. I'm worried a car _____ (run) him over.
4 You _____ (finish) that book! You only bought it yesterday.
5 She _____ (be) really hungry. Did you see how much she ate?
6 I think I _____ (see) this film before but I can't remember.

d Complete the sentences with your own ideas.

1 I can't find my wallet. I think I might _____ *have left it in the shop* _____ .
2 Jane looks really excited. She must _____ .
3 Did he really say that? He must _____ .
4 This band is terrible. They can't _____ .
5 She's half an hour late. I think she might _____ .
6 He never bought her a present in ten years of marriage. He can't _____ .
7 Nobody came to his party. He must _____ .
8 I'm not sure how he crashed the car. He might _____ .

② Pronunciation

★ *have* in *must have / might have / can't have / could have / couldn't have*

a ▶CD3 T28 Listen and complete the sentences.

1 They _____ been disappointed.

2 She _____ left already.

3 I _____ helped you.

4 She _____ gone home.

5 We _____ forgotten to tell him.

6 She _____ seen us.

b ▶CD3 T28 Listen again and repeat the sentences.

③ Grammar

★ Indirect questions

a Circle the correct words.

1 I wonder how old *he is* / *is he*.

2 How old *he is* / *is he*?

3 I can't tell you where *they're* / *are they* from.

4 Where *they're* / *are they* from?

5 I don't understand why *he's* / *is he* unhappy.

6 Why *he's* / *is he* unhappy?

7 I don't know what *we're* / *are we* going to do.

8 What *we're* / *are we* going to do?

b Look at the pictures and complete the sentences.

1 She's wondering ___*who he was*___ .

2 They're not sure _____ _____ .

3 He doesn't know _____ _____ .

4 He doesn't understand _____ _____ .

5 She won't tell him _____ _____ .

6 She wonders _____ _____ .

✱ Indirect questions and auxiliaries

c Finish the sentences with a full stop (.) or a question mark (?).

1 They wanted to know when the train left _____
2 Why are you walking so quickly _____
3 Do you know what I'm thinking _____
4 Where is the nearest police station _____

5 He wondered why she wasn't speaking to him _____
6 I don't know where they are _____
7 What's the problem _____
8 Can you tell me where the toilets are _____

d Complete the questions with the words in the box.

> did she speak to   she spoke to   ~~they live~~
> is it to London   the film starts   do they live
> it is to London   does the film start

1 Can you tell me where _____they live_____ ?
2 Where _____ ?
3 When _____ ?
4 Do you know when _____ ?
5 Who _____ ?
6 Do you happen to know who
_____ ?
7 How far _____ ?
8 Can you tell me how far
_____ ?

e Put the words in the correct order to make questions.

1 need / visa / tell / Can / you / me / I / if / a
Can you tell me if I need a visa? _____

2 need / I / visa / Do / a
_____ ?

3 went / know / you / Do / they / where
_____ ?

4 did / they / go / Where
_____ ?

5 will / back / you / they / when / Do / know / be
_____ ?

6 be / When / back / will / they
_____ ?

4 Vocabulary

✱ Phrasal verbs

a Match the two parts of the sentences. Write a–f in the boxes.

1 He's the managing director now but he started [c]
2 Her hard work paid [ ]
3 She's unhappy because her cat passed [ ]
4 I was a bit scared when the lights went [ ]
5 We didn't have enough players so we had to call [ ]
6 He doesn't really like musicals but we managed to talk [ ]

a him into going with us.
b out because it was really dark.
c out as the office boy.
d off and she came first in the exam.
e off the football match.
f away yesterday.

b Replace the underlined words with the phrasal verbs in the box.

> ~~came across~~   passed away   called off   went out   tied in with

1 I was reading an old school book and I <u>found</u> my first boyfriend's number written in it. *came across*
2 The police are sure he's <u>connected with</u> the robbery. _____
3 They've <u>cancelled</u> the school party because nobody's interested in it. _____
4 My grandfather <u>died</u> peacefully in his sleep. _____
5 We didn't have any more wood and the fire <u>stopped burning</u>. _____

1 We arrived really late because Helen's car _broke_ down.

2 I hadn't seen Jim for years, but I .... into him yesterday by chance.

3 It's a personal thing, so I don't feel like .... into it right now, OK?

4 When we were in England, we .... up some old friends of my parents.

5 I hate it when you put me .... in front of our friends.

6 I've got so much homework to do! It's starting to .... me down.

7 Thanks for inviting me, but I'm afraid I'll have to .... the invitation down.

8 All the hotels were full, but luckily our friends put us .... for the night.

9 Experts are looking .... last week's train crash, to try to find what caused it.

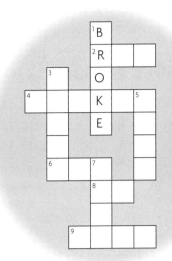

d Complete the sentences with the correct prepositions.

1 Don't worry about looking for that pen. I'm sure it'll turn _up_ somewhere.

2 Look, I hate sport, so there's no way you can talk me .... playing tennis tomorrow!

3 It's a great film. It starts as a thriller, but after about 15 minutes, it turns .... a comedy!

4 I looked on the internet for hours, and then suddenly I came .... something really interesting.

5 I'm afraid my sister's ill, so we have to call .... tomorrow night's party.

6 I asked Sue Jones to go out with me next weekend, but she turned me ....

7 Lots of us were late for school today because the school bus broke .... !

8 I had to give .... dance classes because I haven't got time.

5 **Everyday English**

Circle the correct words.

1 A: I hope I never see Marco again!
   B: Well, look *up / out* – because here he comes now!

2 A: Can you give this to Mary, please?
   B: Sure. I'll give it to her the *time / moment* she gets here.

3 A: What? Pink's coming to play in our town next year?!
   B: No, of course not! *Just / Not* kidding, Maria.

4 A: My dad was really angry when I got home last night.
   B: Serves you *left / right*! If you come home at 3 in the morning, what can you expect?

5 A: I'm really sorry that I'm late.
   B: Don't worry about it! Ten minutes don't matter. *Besides / However*, it's not your fault that the train was late.

6 A: So tell me what Tom said.
   B: No! It's none of your *things / business*! If you really want to know, go and ask Tom himself.

6 Write a story (1)

a Mark's teacher asked him to write a story ending with the words: *That was the last I ever saw of her*. Read his story quickly. Do you think it answers the question successfully?

The snow ¹*fell /* (*was falling*) thick on my windscreen. My eyes were tired from all the whiteness. I wanted to stop but I also wanted to get home. Then I ²*was seeing / saw* her standing by the side of the road.

She got in quickly. She ³*shivered / was shivering* from the cold. We soon started talking. She told me that she lived in the next town and then she told me about how her husband ⁴*was killed / had been killed* in a car crash on this very road, exactly one year ago.

Then suddenly she ⁵*was screaming / screamed* 'Look out!' I looked and saw the car in front of me. I put on the brakes, the car skidded across the road and came to a stop. I ⁶*was shaking / shook* with fear. I turned to thank her because she

⁷*saved / had saved* my life. However, when I looked round she ⁸*went / had gone* and her door was open. I looked out and saw a dark figure ⁹*walk / walking* in the distance. It soon disappeared in the snow. That was the last I ever saw of her.

b Mark uses a variety of past tenses in his story. (Circle) the correct words.

WRITING TIP

Developing your ideas to write a story (1)

A Getting ideas is an extremely important part of writing a story. Let your imagination take control. Close your eyes and write down any ideas that come into your mind.

Ask yourself questions and write down your answers. Here are some examples for the story in Exercise 7.

Who was she? *A girlfriend, a ghost, a mysterious stranger ...*

Why was I with her? *She asked me for directions, I was seeing her off on a plane, I picked her up hitchhiking ...*

Why did I never see her again? *She went to live in another country, she disappeared, she died, she gave me her phone number but I lost it ...*

B Use the combination you like best to create an outline to the story.

I was driving. I stopped to pick a woman hitchhiker up. We started talking. I didn't see the car in the middle of the road. She screamed to warn me. I didn't crash. I looked at her. Her door was open. I saw a figure walking along the road. It disappeared.

C Now ask yourself questions to develop the story. For example:
  - What was the weather like?
  - Where was I going?
  - How was I feeling?
  - Why did I stop?
  - What did we talk about?

D Use the answers to these questions to develop your story. Remember:
  - use a good range of vocabulary (adjectives, adverbs, etc.) to make your story descriptive
  - show a good command of past tenses
  - link your sentences and paragraphs well.

---

c Write a story ending with the words: *And then the phone rang*.

Unit check

1 Fill in the spaces

Complete the text with the words in the box.

| between   have   wonder   might   message |
| neither   we are   ~~can't~~   must   most |

There .... *can't* .... be many people who have never heard of the Bermuda Triangle. This area of sea
[1] .... Florida and Bermuda is one of the world's [2] .... mysterious places.

Over a hundred ships and planes have been lost here. Many of these [3] .... have been in accidents
or storms. But [4] .... of these causes explain the mystery of Flight 19 – a US Navy training flight
from Fort Lauderdale with the most modern technology. The radio operator back at base [5] ....
have thought it was strange when he received a [6] .... from the pilot saying they were lost and
that the sky seemed strange. His last communication was: 'I don't know where [7] .... It looks like
we ...'. They were never seen again. Many people [8] .... why the flight disappeared so suddenly.
Some think it must [9] .... been caught in a tropical storm.

9

2 Choose the correct answers

Circle the correct answer: a, b or c.

1 She .... liked it. She left after 20 minutes.
   a must have   b might have   c (can't have)

2 We're coming to your city next week. Can you
   put us .... for one or two nights, please?
   a up   b down   c in

3 Do you happen to know where .... ?
   a they went   b did they go   c went they

4 I was in bed when the lights went ....
   a over   b about   c out

5 He might .... phoned but I wasn't in.
   a has   b had   c have

6 A window was broken at school today. I'm sure
   James Gordon was tied .... with it.
   a off   b up   c in

7 I wonder why .... that.
   a she said   b said she   c did she say

8 I was looking for my keys and I .... across
   €10 behind the sofa.
   a found   b came   c went

9 There .... have been 80,000 people at the
   game. It was so crowded.
   a can't   b must   c might

8

3 Vocabulary

Change the underlined words. Use the correct form of the verbs in brackets and a preposition.

1 My friend's uncle died last week. (pass) *passed away*

2 Suddenly, at midnight, all the lights in the house stopped working. (go) ....

3 I met my mother's best friend at the cinema last night. (run) ....

4 Sorry I'm late. The train stopped working. (break) ....

5 The pitch was covered in water, so they cancelled the match. (call) ....

6 Do you remember that I lost my schoolbag? Well, it appeared in the garage! (turn) ....

7 I was reading a magazine yesterday, and I found an interesting article. (come) ....

8 He invited me to a concert but I said no to his invitation. (turn) ....

9 My brother and his girlfriend ended their relationship yesterday. (break) ....

8

How did you do?

Total: **25**

😊	Very good 20 – 25	😐	OK 14 – 19	🙁	Review Unit 10 again 0 – 13

11 Love

1 Grammar

✱ Reported speech review

a Rewrite the sentences in direct speech.

1 The man told the woman that he was really scared of dogs.
'_I'm really scared of dogs_____,' the man told her.

2 Sue told her father that she would go to the cinema with him on Saturday.
'_____,' Sue told her father.

3 John explained he had to get up early in the morning to catch the train.
'_____,' explained John.

4 Janet told us there had been an earthquake in China.
'_____,' Janet told us.

5 Dad said he was sorry he couldn't get home earlier.
'_____,' said Dad.

6 Ben told us he was going to France in the morning.
'_____,' Ben told us.

7 Anna said she had to leave before eight o'clock.
'_____,' said Anna.

8 Marek said that he couldn't type very fast.
'_____,' said Marek.

b Rewrite the sentences. Use the words in brackets.

1 'You must buy your girlfriend some flowers,' Mum said. (that)
Mum _told me that I had to buy___ some flowers for my girlfriend.

2 'Tony is my brother, not my boyfriend,' Anne said. (was)
Anne _____ her brother, not her boyfriend.

3 'I did not steal the money,' the man said. (said)
The man _____ the money.

4 'I can't go on holiday in August,' Tony said. (explained)
Tony _____ on holiday in August.

5 'I have not learned anything for the test,' Jane said to us. (told)
Jane _____ _____ anything for the test.

6 'I'm going to marry Cathy,' Nick said. (he)
Nick told us that _____ .

7 'I don't want to hear complaints all the time,' the headmaster said. (said)
The headmaster _____ hear complaints all the time.

8 'I promise to give you the money back in three days' time,' he said to me. (would)
He promised that he _____ the money back in three days' time.

2 Grammar

⭑ Reported questions

a Put the questions into reported speech.

1 'When is your birthday?' (The girl wanted to know ...)

   The girl wanted to know when my birthday was.

2 'Will we get to the concert on time?' (Jane asked ...)

   ....

3 'Can you install this game for me?' (Carol asked me ...)

   ....

4 'Why can't I stay up longer?' (My little sister asked ...)

   ....

5 'Where's the hospital?' (The driver wanted to know ...)

   ....

6 'Have you been to Canada?' (He asked me ...)

   ....

b Complete the conversation with the phrases in the box.

> don't think   was brilliant   doesn't mean   I'll go
> ~~Have you seen~~   Why's that   it was awful

Lucy: *Have you seen* Matrix Revolutions?

Liz: No, I haven't, and I ¹............................. I want to.

Lucy: ²............................. ?

Liz: My friends have seen it, and they said

   ³............................. .

Lucy: I find that surprising. I've only seen the first part, and
   that ⁴............................. .

Liz: I know, but that ⁵............................. much!

Lucy: You're probably right, but I think ⁶.............................
   and see it anyway.

c Complete the report on the conversation between Lucy and Liz.

Lucy asked Liz ....*whether*....... she had seen Matrix
Revolutions. Liz replied that she ¹............................. , but
she ²............................. want to. Lucy ³.............................
to know why. Liz replied that her friends ⁴.............................
it, and they ⁵............................. awful. Lucy answered that
she ⁶............................. that surprising. She ⁷.............................
the first part, and that ⁸............................. brilliant. Liz
replied that she ⁹............................. , but that
¹⁰............................. much. Lucy replied that she
¹¹............................. right, but she ¹²............................. and
see it anyway.

3 Vocabulary

⭑ Appearance

Robert

Donna

Kevin

Jenny

a Write the names of the people.

1 Who is plump? ....*Kevin*.......

2 Who has got a ponytail?

   ....

3 Who has got a double chin?

   ....

4 Who has got wrinkles on his
   forehead? ....

5 Who is clean shaven? ....

6 Who has got freckles on her
   cheek? ....

b Look at the pictures again and
complete the sentences.

1 Robert has got .... on
   his face. He is rather short, but
   ....*slim*....... .

2 Jenny has got .... hair.
   She is slim, but she has got
   a .... chin.

3 Donna has got her hair in a
   .... On her left arm,
   she's got a .... of
   a dolphin.

4 Kevin has got ....
   eyebrows. He has got
   .... hair, a ....
   and .... on his forehead.

4 Vocabulary

✱ Personality

Complete the text. (Circle) the correct answer: a, b, c or d.

I've got three sisters and two brothers. My oldest brother is Adam. Once I was ill for two weeks. Adam was really ¹ _considerate_ and looked after me very well. But sometimes Adam is really ² _____ . He likes to tell us what to do all the time and how we should do it. We often tell him to be more ³ _____ , but he doesn't listen. Ernest, my other brother, is the most ⁴ _____ of us all. He was always the best student in his class, and he finished university really quickly. The problem is that he never has any time for himself, but we tell him to be a little less ⁵ _____ and relax a bit more. We all get on really well with my youngest sister Margaret, except when we try to interfere with her life. She is a very ⁶ _____ person: she really doesn't like other people to tell her what to do!

1	a	(considerate)	b	ambitious	c	determined	d	imaginative
2	a	sensitive	b	independent	c	bossy	d	ambitious
3	a	imaginative	b	bossy	c	ambitious	d	considerate
4	a	bossy	b	ambitious	c	sensitive	d	insensitive
5	a	determined	b	imaginative	c	sensitive	d	considerate
6	a	independent	b	insensitive	c	considerate	d	sensitive

5 Grammar

✱ Reporting verbs

a (Circle) the correct verbs.

Tracey and Caroline were talking about going to the cinema. Tracey ¹*said* / *told* that she ²*wanted* / *wants* to see a thriller. Caroline ³*said* / *told* that she ⁴*will* / *would* like to see a romantic film. Tracey ⁵*said* / *offered* to go and get a programme. Caroline ⁶*suggested* / *asked* checking the programme on the internet. She went online, but some minutes later she ⁷*said* / *told* that there ⁸*aren't* / *weren't* any interesting films on. Tracey ⁹*said* / *told* Caroline that it ¹⁰*might* / *will* be better to rent a DVD and watch it at home. So Caroline ¹¹*asked* / *said* her to go and get a good DVD. Tracey ¹²*said* / *told* that she ¹³*is* / *was* happy to do that. Twenty minutes later she came back. She ¹⁴*apologised* / *complained* for choosing a thriller, but Caroline ¹⁵*refused* / *invited* to watch it!

b Use the past tense form of the verbs in the box to write the sentences in reported speech.

explain ~~tell~~ refuse persuade beg suggest agree apologise

1 'Wash your hands before you sit down!' Mum said to my little brother.

Mum told my little brother to wash his hands before _he sat down._

2 'Please, please lend me your DVD player!' Pete said to me.

----

3 'I'm really sorry that I forgot about your birthday,' Cathy said to her dad.

----

4 'All right – I'll make pizza for supper,' my mother said.

----

5 'I'm late because of the traffic,' she said.

----

6 'I won't do it!' she said.

----

7 **Tom:** 'I know you don't like football, but please will you watch the match with me, just for once?'

Alan: 'Oh, all right then. But just this once!'

Tom --

8 'Let's play tennis,' said Lucy.

----

6 Pronunciation

✱ Intonation in reported questions

a ▶CD3 T29 Listen and repeat.

1 What's your favourite colour?

2 How are you enjoying the meal?

3 When will you be back?

4 Do you often watch TV?

b ▶CD3 T30 Listen and repeat.

1 He asked me what my favourite colour was.

2 We asked them how they were enjoying the meal.

3 He asked her when she'd be back.

4 He asked me if I often watched TV.

7 Fiction in mind

a Read another extract from *Two Lives* by Helen Naylor. What is Huw's profession?

On one of his many walks, he read Megan's letter for the twentieth time. She said she was still Megan Jenkins. 'So,' Huw thought, 'she never got married.' He remembered her as a warm, loving and intelligent person and thought that it was sad that she had never shared all this with a man. Then he laughed at himself. 'Maybe she was happy to be single,' he thought. 'Or maybe she was married and something happened and she changed her name back to Jenkins. What does it matter? It's all in the past now.'

When he arrived back home that evening he told his family that he had made a decision: he was not going to write back to Megan. His life was here now. Better to let the past stay in the past.

Later in the evening, Huw went back upstairs to his studio and, for some reason, started looking through some of his early work. There were paintings and drawings of his that he hadn't looked at for years. He found some drawings he'd done in the first few months after he'd arrived in Toronto. Most of them were of ships. He remembered he used to think about getting on one of the ships and sailing away. Sometimes he had wanted to sail back to Wales and Megan, and then later he'd just wanted to escape anywhere.

He spent the next few hours lost in his thoughts. It was five o'clock in the morning when he looked at his watch and slowly went to bed, his head still full of the past.

(from Naylor H. *Two Lives* CUP, p. 32.)

b Read the text again. All these statements are true. Underline the parts of the text which tell you the same thing.

1 Huw had read the letter before.

2 He had nice memories of Megan.

3 Huw decided something and then told other people.

4 Huw didn't want to think about things in the past.

5 Huw wasn't sure why he started to look at his early paintings.

6 Before, Huw had dreams of going to another place by ship.

7 Huw thought about these things for a long time.

8 When he went to bed, Huw was still thinking about his earlier life.

To find out if Huw goes back to Wales to find Megan – read the story!

Skills in mind

8 Read

Read the article. For each question (circle) the correct answer.

Romeo and Juliet:
the greatest love story of all time

Since the invention of the motion picture in 1894, *Romeo and Juliet* has been one of the most popular stories in films. Numerous movies have been based on Shakespeare's famous love story, the earliest dating back to 1900.

Many directors have taken this famous play and made it into a film, trying to keep to the themes of the original story. One of them is Baz Luhrmann. His version of Romeo and Juliet, produced in 1996, has been described as an original, post-modern version of Shakespeare's tragic love story.

With this extremely successful film, Luhrmann has managed to update the story – by combining modern-day settings and characters with almost the original language. The story is set in Miami. The changes in the language, together with dramatic gun fights and passionate love scenes, make the story more accessible to modern audiences.

In Luhrmann's version of the film, the main characters, Romeo (Leonardo DiCaprio) and Juliet (Clare Danes), are Miami teenagers of the nineties. Even though the setting of the film is very unconventional, it contains all the themes of the original version, because it does not change the story at all.

1 Lots of films have been produced that are based on
   a William Shakespeare's play *Romeo and Juliet*.
   b a motion picture from 1894 called *Romeo and Juliet*.
   c an invention made by William Shakespeare in 1894.

2 Baz Luhrmann
   a is the only film director who has tried to keep to the themes of the original play.
   b is one of the film directors who have tried to keep to the themes of the original play.
   c produced his earliest version of *Romeo and Juliet* as early as 1900.

3 The language in Luhrmann's film is
   a exactly the same as in Shakespeare's play.
   b completely different from Shakespeare's play.
   c almost the same as in Shakespeare's play.

4 Why did Luhrmann make some changes to the setting?
   a Because he added gun fights and passionate love scenes.
   b Because he wanted to help people to understand the story better.
   c Because teenagers in Miami speak a very strong dialect.

5 Which of the following statements is true about Baz Luhrmann?
   a He produced a successful, but unconventional and provocative version of the play.
   b He produced a modern, but not very successful version of the play.
   c He produced a successful modern version of the play.

Unit check

1 Fill in the spaces

Complete the text with the words in the box.

> ~~slim~~ cropped bad-tempered sensitive hair tattoo fit ambitious determined ponytail

My best friend is Carolyn. A year ago she started to exercise regularly, and now she's really _____slim_____ .
She also changed her hairstyle. First she had long [1]_____ which she wore in a [2]_____ , but
now her hair's [3]_____ . Carolyn's the best student in my class. She's really [4]_____ , and
sometimes she gets a bit [5]_____ when she doesn't get top marks. But I like Carolyn a lot. When I
have a problem, she's very [6]_____ . I want to learn from Carolyn. I'm going to exercise regularly too.
I'm very [7]_____ and I won't give up before I am as [8]_____ as her. But one thing's for sure: I'm
not going to get a [9]_____ on my left arm. That's something I don't like so much about her! | 9 |

2 Choose the correct answers

(Circle) the correct answer: a, b or c.

1 Jane said that she _____ nervous.
   a (was) b were c be

2 She asked me if I _____ seen her glasses.
   a have been b having c had

3 Your sister said that she _____ to leave.
   a had b having c have

4 John promised that he _____ study the words.
   a to b would c would to

5 They wanted to know when he _____ back.
   a would come b will coming c would

6 I asked them if they _____ help me.
   a be able to b able c could

7 They apologised for not _____ on time.
   a being b to be c been

8 We asked them _____ us an email.
   a writing b write c to write

9 I suggested _____ Peter for some advice.
   a asking b to ask c ask | 8 |

3 Vocabulary

In each line, underline the word which does not belong in the group.

	a		b		c		d	
1	a	considerate	b	long	c	bossy	d	sensitive
2	a	bad-tempered	b	bossy	c	considerate	d	insensitive
3	a	wavy	b	long	c	cropped	d	plump
4	a	fringe	b	tattoo	c	scar	d	freckles
5	a	beard	b	moustache	c	clean-shaven	d	well-built
6	a	slim	b	spiky	c	plump	d	well-built
7	a	medium-height	b	tall	c	straight	d	short
8	a	spots	b	freckles	c	wrinkles	d	eyelashes
9	a	ponytail	b	fringe	c	highlights	d	wrinkles

| 8 |

How did you do?

Total: | 25 |

| | Very good 20 – 25 | | OK 14 – 19 | | Review Unit 11 again 0 – 13 |

12 Regret

1 Grammar

✱ Third conditional

a Match the sentences with the pictures a–d. Write 1–4 in the boxes.

1 If she'd studied harder for the test, she would have got a better mark.

2 If she hadn't studied hard for the test, she wouldn't have got such a good mark.

3 If we'd left earlier, we wouldn't have missed the train.

4 If we'd left any later, we would have missed the train.

b Complete the third conditional sentences with the correct form of the verbs.

1 I don't think so many people _would have come_ (come) to the concert if they _'d known_ (know) that the lead singer was ill.

2 What _____ you _____ (say) if I _____ (show) you the present earlier?

3 We _____ (save) a lot of money if we _____ (go) to a cheaper restaurant.

4 He _____ (not buy) such an expensive guitar if his father _____ (not give) him the money.

5 If she _____ (pass) her driving test, she _____ (drive) us to Italy.

6 Nobody _____ (hear) us if we _____ (not shout).

7 If you _____ (not run after) me, I _____ (not fall).

8 Why _____ he _____ (phone) us if he _____ (not be) in trouble?

c Match the sentences below with the pictures a–g. Write 1–7 in the boxes. Then join the sentences using the third conditional.

 7

1 One of Daniel's friends gave Daniel his ticket for a concert.

2 Daniel went to the concert.

3 He was standing next to a girl called Annie.

4 Annie and Daniel had a chat.

5 The next evening, Daniel and Annie went out together.

6 They fell in love.

7 A year later they got married.

If one of Daniel's friends hadn't given Daniel his ticket, he wouldn't have gone to the concert. If Daniel hadn't gone to ...

2 Grammar

✳ I wish / If only for past situations

Write down a regret for each situation, starting your sentences with *I wish* or *If only*.
Use an expression from the box for each sentence.

kick ball	drive so fast	break vase	play with pen	~~slam door~~	buy sports car

1 *I wish I hadn't slammed the door.*

The neighbours are really annoyed.

2 _____

Where can I buy a new one now?

3 _____

What will my parents say?

4 _____

I'll never get rid of the stain on my jeans!

5 _____

This is going to cost me money.

6 _____

I have no money left.

3 Grammar

✳ should / shouldn't have done

a Match the two parts of the sentences. Write a–f in the boxes.

1 I should listen to my parents
2 I should have listened to my parents
3 I shouldn't have been angry with Jane
4 I shouldn't be angry with Jane
5 I should write her an email
6 I should have written her an email

d	a because I think they were right.
	b because it wasn't her fault.
	c before it is too late.
	d because I think they are right.
	e before it was too late.
	f because it isn't her fault.

b Write a response to these statements using *should've* or *shouldn't have* and a phrase from the box with the correct form of the verb.

~~leave earlier~~
call the police
take a jumper with her
take the risk
wear better shoes
buy something earlier

1 I missed the bus. *You should've left earlier.*
2 She's feeling cold. _____
3 He lost all his money. _____
4 They can't find a present for their mum. _____
5 They saw that the man had a gun. _____
6 He slipped on the pavement and broke his leg. _____

4 Pronunciation

✱ *should / shouldn't have*

a ▶ **CD3 T31** Listen and repeat.

1 You shouldn't have done that.
2 I shouldn't have listened to her.
3 I gave it back to her, but I shouldn't have.
4 We should have bought it.
5 They didn't tell us but they should have.
6 You should have written to me.

b ▶ **CD3 T31** Listen again. <u>Underline</u> *shouldn't have* when it is pronounced fully. Circle it when it is pronounced quickly and sounds like 'shouldenev'.

5 Vocabulary

✱ Anger

a Complete the text. Circle the correct word: a, b, c or d.

A few weeks ago I wanted to go on a bike tour with three friends. The evening before the tour Jeremy and Laura called to say they couldn't come. I was [1] _furious_ . I was especially [2] _____ with Jeremy because he was the one who had initially suggested going for the bike tour. Anyway, the next morning I was sorry for losing my [3] _____ and rang up Jeremy to apologize. But he didn't even want to talk. He was so [4] _____ ! I [5] _____ my cool and said, "OK. If you're so [6] _____ and lose your temper so easily, it's your problem and not mine!" You know what? He started having [7] _____ and bit [8] _____ for 'shouting at him'! I don't know what he meant! But what could I do? I think I can only [9] _____ and wait for him to cool down again!

	a	b	c	d
1	~~furious~~	hot-headed	mad at	calm
2	hot-headed	temper	cross	mad
3	head	tantrum	calm	temper
4	cool	hot-headed	upset	calm
5	got	had	kept	bit
6	indignant	calm	cool	hot-headed
7	a temper	a tantrum	my head off	his cool
8	my head off	a tantrum	his cool	his temper
9	be calm	have a tantrum	be cross	bite his head off

b (**Vocabulary bank**) Read the dialogue and <u>underline</u> the correct words.

Will: Hey, Joe? What's up? You look pretty [1] <u>upset</u> / *bitter*.

Joe: Nothing really. I just had a [2] *hot / heated* argument with Rachel.

Will: Not again. What was it about this time?

Joe: Music. She basically told me that all the music I like is rubbish.

Will: That's a bit rude.

Joe: Well at first I think she was joking, just saying silly things. But after a while I got a bit [3] *mad / irritated*. So I tried to change the subject. But she wouldn't stop. So I told her that she didn't know anything about music and that all the CDs in her collection were just there because her ex-boyfriends had bought them for her. Well then she gave me a really [4] *grey / black* look and acted all [5] *indignant / bitter* as if I'd said something really unfair. She wanted ME to say sorry to her.

Will: So what did you do?

Joe: Well I acted [6] *irritated / outraged*. I wanted her to feel that she had made me really angry.

Will: Did it work?

Joe: Not really. She just walked off in a really [7] *foul / angry* mood.

Will: So what are you going to do?

Joe: Nothing. I'll wait a while. Then next time I see her she'll pretend to be [8] *bitter / indignant* and let me know that she hasn't forgotten. And then we'll find something new to argue about. Same as always.

Will: Well, I suppose that's what sisters are for.

Joe: Exactly.

6 Study help

✱ How to complete cloze texts

Sometimes you have to fill in the spaces in a text with one word and no clues are given.

- It's important that you read the whole text first. Don't focus on the spaces – try to understand what the general meaning of the text is. Look at the title too!

- Carefully study the words before and after the space. Try to find clues that help you to identify the meaning of the word needed. Is it the opposite of something? Is it an example of something? Is it a synonym? Is it part of an expression?

- Try to identify the type of word that's needed. For example, is it an article? A preposition? A noun? Look at number 2 in the text below. The words before the space are: *can be caused*. This tells us that the sentence is a present simple passive construction. The words after the space tell us what the cause is, so what is the missing word?

- If the word you need to fill in is a verb, make sure it agrees with the subject that it goes with. Don't forget the third person *-s*!

- If you are not sure about a word, try to guess the answer and note it down on a piece of paper. Then come back later to the spaces you found difficult to do. You will sometimes find it easier to find the right word the second time round.

- Read the whole text again and check that the words you have filled in make sense.

Complete the text with one word for each space.

What is anger?
And what can you do about it?

According to psychologists, anger
[1] _____*is*_____ a feeling. As with other emotional states, we notice changes when we are angry. There are biological changes, for example. Our heart rate and blood pressure go up, as do the levels of our energy hormones.

Anger can be caused [2] _____ both external and internal events. You could be angry at a specific [3] _____ , such as a classmate or a teacher, or perhaps an event. For example, maybe you have [4] _____ your bus, or it starts raining and you [5] _____ planned to go for a walk. Or your anger could be caused by worrying [6] _____ your personal problems. Memories of very negative events can also trigger angry feelings.

However, you can control your angry feelings with simple techniques. There are books and courses [7] _____ can teach you relaxation techniques, and once you have learned the techniques you can use them in different situations. If you are in a relationship where both of you are quick-tempered, it might be a good idea for both of you [8] _____ learn these techniques. Practise these techniques daily and learn to use [9] _____ when you're in a difficult situation.

7 Write a story (2)

a John's teacher asked him to write a story with the title: 'An embarrassing situation'. Read his answer. Why was the situation embarrassing?

An embarrassing situation

I was on holiday with two of my friends and we were staying in a hotel.[1] The football World Cup was starting and we all wanted to watch it. We decided to watch it in my room, because there was a TV there, but we just couldn't get a picture. We tried everything but we couldn't sort it out.[2]

Finally,[3] we decided to phone someone in reception and ask them to look at it. When the man arrived, he looked at the TV and calmly switched it on, before taking the remote control and pressing the button for the right channel![4]

b The writer gives the events, but the text does not contain much detail, so it isn't very interesting. Read the question prompts. Think of answers to them and write them down.

1 Where was the holiday? When? What was the place like? What was the hotel like?

2 How did you feel when you noticed that the TV didn't work? Why?

3 How long did you wait before you called reception? Had the match already started?

4 How did you feel when you realised you hadn't noticed the TV was not switched on? Did you later tell your friends about what had happened? Why? / Why not?

c Rewrite the text using the ideas you wrote in Exercise 7b to make it more interesting.

d Write a story with the title *A dangerous journey*.

Unit check

1 Fill in the spaces

Complete the text with the words in the box.

| furious | ~~letter~~ | keep | regretting | hot-headed | difficult | temper | work | tantrum | mad |

Dear Jane,

Thank you for your ___letter___ . I'm afraid it's really not very easy to advise you. You had a fight with your boyfriend and lost your ¹_____ , and now you are ²_____ it. You say in your letter that your boyfriend is quite a ³_____ person, but it seems that it is ⁴_____ for you to ⁵_____ your cool too. Now you are ⁶_____ with him, but maybe you should understand that he is also ⁷_____ at you. Perhaps you could learn to relax a bit more and avoid having a ⁸_____ when you are arguing with someone you like. Maybe you can ⁹_____ something out together.

Yours, Barbara

[9]

2 Choose the correct answers

(Circle) the correct answer: a, b or c.

1 If I _____ ill, I would have gone to school.
   a (hadn't been) b were not c am not

2 They would not _____ in love if they hadn't met.
   a fall b had fallen c have fallen

3 If the police hadn't come, the man would have _____ .
   a escaping b escaped c escape

4 He's going to hit you! Look _____ !
   a in b out c under

5 I'm so curious. I wish I _____ her before.
   a asked b been asked c had asked

6 I missed the bus. I _____ left so late.
   a hadn't b should have c shouldn't have

7 We should have left before they _____ .
   a arrived b would arrive c arrive

8 This is so complicated, I don't think we can _____ it out.
   a sort b stop c avoid

9 I am so full! If only I _____ so much.
   a not eaten b wouldn't have eaten
   c hadn't eaten

[8]

3 Vocabulary

Replace the underlined words so that the sentences make sense.

1 I don't know what I said to Jo, but she bit my arm off. ___head___

2 In an emergency, you should try to keep your calm. _____

3 My dad is really heat-headed.

   _____

4 Mr Riley lost his mood today.

   _____

5 Ben is in a black mood today.

   _____

6 I forgot Valentine's Day and my girlfriend is temper. _____

7 Amy doesn't like me. She always gives me a foul look. _____

8 They started a(n) irritated argument because of football. _____

9 When Mum said he couldn't have an ice cream, Tim had a temper.

   _____ [8]

How did you do?

Total: [25]

| 😊 | Very good 20 – 25 | 😐 | OK 14 – 19 | 🙁 | Review Unit 12 again 0 – 13 |

13 Hopes and fears

1 Grammar

✱ Non-defining relative clauses (giving extra information)

a Complete the sentences with the correct relative clause in the box.

where her family have a restaurant	which I have read five times
which is not far from San Francisco	which was why I couldn't go to school
who is still very popular	which I know I wrote down
~~where you can find beautiful beaches~~	whose name I've forgotten

1 I love going on holiday to Ireland, __*where you can find beautiful beaches*__ .

2 Madonna, _____, had her first hit in the 1980s.

3 Karen's best friend, _____, comes from China.

4 She lives in London, _____.

5 I had a nasty cold, _____.

6 *The Lord of the Rings*, _____, is my favourite book.

7 He is Californian and was born in Santa Cruz, _____.

8 I've lost your address, _____.

b Complete the text with *who*, *whose*, *which* or *where*.

Mark O'Brian, __*who*__ **was on his way to work early last Tuesday morning, was driving down North Lane when he was shocked by something he saw.**

A driver, ¹_____ must have driven down the same street only a few minutes before, had lost control of his car. The car, ²_____ had landed on its roof, burst into flames immediately.

Mr O'Brian, ³_____ quick thinking helped save the driver's life, got out of his car and saw that there was a man in the driver's seat. Mark phoned the fire brigade and then ran back to his own car, ⁴_____ he kept a fire extinguisher. He rushed back to the scene just as another man was approaching.

O'Brian and the other man, ⁵_____ has not been seen since the accident, managed to put out the fire.

They then broke the passenger window with a stone and freed the driver, ⁶_____ luckily was not seriously injured. He was taken to hospital, ⁷_____ his condition has been described as 'comfortable'.

c Join the sentences using *who*, *which*, *where* or *whose*. Sometimes you will need to change the order of the clauses. You will not need the underlined words.

1 Joanne speaks six languages. <u>She</u> lives next door.

   Joanne, who lives next door, speaks six languages.

2 I love scuba diving in the Indian Ocean. You can still find a lot of attractive fish <u>there</u>.

   _____

3 Next month Stephanie will move to London. Her partner has a flat <u>there</u>.

   _____

4 Alex is getting married next year. <u>His</u> sister studies with me.

   _____

5 Gemma has won the lottery. <u>She</u> lives next door to me.

   _____

6 My new computer is fantastic. I got <u>it</u> for a very good price.

   _____

2 Grammar and pronunciation

✷ Defining vs. non-defining relative clauses

a Tick (✔) if the sentence is correct. If the sentence is wrong, write a cross (✘) and insert or remove the commas.

1 Flying which so many people are afraid of is actually the safest way to travel. **✘**

Flying, which so many people are afraid of,
is actually the safest way to travel.

2 She's the girl that I told you about. ☐

3 He's the actor, that's afraid of clowns. ☐

4 Where's the huge spider that was in the bathroom earlier? ☐

5 I have to deliver this newspaper to number 13 where that big dog lives. ☐

6 Isn't she the actress, who's afraid of butterflies? ☐

7 My dad is allergic to cats which are my favourite animals. ☐

8 That's the man whose dog bit my brother. ☐

b ▶ CD3 T32 Listen to the sentences in Exercise 2a and check your answers. Where can you hear the pauses?

c ▶ CD3 T32 Listen again and repeat the sentences.

3 Vocabulary

✷ Adjectives with prefixes

a Complete the text with the correct forms of the adjectives in brackets. One of the adjectives stays the same.

Here are two things I hope will change in the future. The first one is about some of the people that I work with at the tourist information office. They're so ¹ *unhelpful* (helpful)! It's embarrassing sometimes, how ² .... (polite) they can be to visitors from other countries. Even my boss gets ³ .... (patient) sometimes when people can't speak English well. It makes me feel really ⁴ .... (comfortable).

Secondly, I want all the ⁵ .... (responsible) people in the world to stop destroying our planet. Too many politicians seem to be ⁶ .... (concerned) about pollution and cutting down trees. I wish countries would make it ⁷ .... (legal) to do things like this. It's so ⁸ .... (healthy) for our future. I suppose this is just an ⁹ .... (possible) dream, though, and I'm ¹⁰ .... (afraid) it will never happen.

b **Vocabulary bank** Complete the dialogues with the opposite forms of the adjectives in the box. There are two words you won't need.

sincere   rational   able   ~~personal~~   attractive   complete   probable   literate   mature   modest

1 A: She's not a very warm human being, is she?   B: No, she's very ___*impersonal*___ .
2 A: Does she ever mean what she says?   B: No, she's really _____ .
3 A: He's a great actor, but he's not good-looking.   B: He is very _____ .
4 A: Did Beethoven finish his tenth symphony?   B: No, it was _____ .
5 A: Her fear of gloves just doesn't make sense.   B: Yes, it's quite _____ .
6 A: Do you think Malta will ever win the World Cup? B: It's highly _____ .
7 A: Did you hear those stupid jokes he told?   B: I know. He's so _____ .
8 A: Can he read or write?   B: No, he's _____ .

4 Grammar

✱ Definite, indefinite and zero article

a Complete the sentences with *the*, *a* or *ø* (nothing).

1 I have ___*a*___ shower at least once a day.

2 This is _____ new school that I told you about.

3 His brother works as _____ pilot for British Airways.

4 Lidia plays _____ drums in a band.

5 If he doesn't feel better tomorrow, we'll have to take him to _____ hospital.

6 Can you pass me _____ sugar, please?

7 When does _____ match start?

8 I'm allergic to _____ school!

b Tick (✓) if the line is correct. If the line has an article (*a*, *an*, or *the*) which should not be there, write the word in the space.

Yesterday my friend Linda and I had lunch at the pizzeria	1	✔
behind our school. I know Linda is not keen on ~~the~~ pizza,	2	*the*
but I think she came along because of me. At the table next to us	3	___
there were two guys from our class. The one of them was really funny.	4	___
He tried to imitate all the people in the pizzeria. We couldn't stop	5	___
laughing. But there were some the customers who did not like	6	___
the fact that two boys were imitating them. They complained to	7	___
the owner of the restaurant and he came over and told them to stop.	8	___
It was a real pity because Linda and I were really having a fun!	9	___

5 Vocabulary

✱ Phrasal verbs with *through*

Complete the sentences with the correct form of phrasal verbs with *through*.

1 Good news! I managed to ___*get through*___ to the final of the badminton competition.

2 I just can't _____ another of Uncle Ted's holiday videos! They're so boring!

3 I _____ my driving test – I didn't make a single mistake!

4 I need to _____ my notes tonight. I've got an important test tomorrow.

5 OK, I'll _____ it all one more time. Starting from the beginning, ...

6 Culture in mind

▶ CD3 T33 **Listen to part of an article about triskaidekaphobia. Answer the questions.**

1 What is triskaidekaphobia?
2 What does Michael Ballack always wear?
3 What will Stephen King <u>not</u> do when he gets to page 49 of a book?
4 How many more people were involved in traffic accidents on Friday 13th compared to Friday 6th?

b Read the rest of the article about the number thirteen. Write 'L' (lucky), 'U' (unlucky) or 'N' (neither lucky nor unlucky) to show what the number means to the people in the table.

Ancient Egyptians	L	Chinese	
Christians		Sikhs	
Norse gods		Wiccans	

triskaidekaphobia

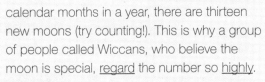

Having thirteen people to dinner is often <u>regarded as</u> especially unlucky, with one guest likely to die <u>within a year</u>. There are religious reasons for this belief. In medieval times, Christians <u>pointed out</u> that in the Last Supper, Christ was betrayed by the thirteenth 'dinner guest', Judas; ancient Norse mythology tells the story of the murder of Balder, one of the eleven gods invited to Odin's Valhalla Banquet, by Loki, the god of evil (and the thirteenth person at the table.)

Another reason why thirteen is special could be <u>related to</u> the moon. Although there are, of course, twelve calendar months in a year, there are thirteen new moons (try counting!). This is why a group of people called Wiccans, who believe the moon is special, <u>regard</u> the number so <u>highly</u>.

In the Punjabi and Hindi languages, the word thirteen also means 'yours', making it a very positive number, especially in the Sikh culture. And in Ancient Egypt, they considered the 13th stage of life to be death (or 'afterlife', a good thing).

The number thirteen is not significant everywhere, though. In China, Japan and Korea, the number four can sound like the word for 'death', and <u>consequently</u> buildings sometimes either do not have a fourth floor, or lifts mark it 'F' instead of four.

c Match the words below with <u>underlined</u> parts of the text.

1 have a good opinion of   _regard ... highly_
2 so   ....
3 thought to be   ....
4 connected with   ....
5 made sure people knew   ....

Skills in mind

7 Listen

▶ CD3 T34 Listen to an interview with a psychologist about why people like frightening stories and the effect such stories can have on people. What does the psychologist say? Take notes to complete the sentences.

1 People like telling frightening stories so they can
   ...*entertain others*... .

2 Most of the stories have a

   ....

3 If a story has comic relief, we

   ....

4 Healthy adult people are not harmed by listening to frightening stories because

   ....

5 Fairy tales are important for children because

   ....

6 A child who listens to fairy tales also

   ....

7 Some horror films are

   ....

LISTENING TIP

Note taking

- Before you listen, first read the task carefully. It gives you important information about what to expect in the listening. Then read through the questions. You may want to <u>underline</u> key words in the questions. Look at the instructions for Exercise 7. What are the key words?

- Try to predict what kinds of answers you are expected to give. Does the question ask for some specific information (for example, a person's age, or physical appearance)? What kind of language might you need to answer the question?

- Listen carefully to the information given.

- Write clear answers that are not too long, but have all the necessary information. Use abbreviations (*16* instead of *sixteen*, *km* instead of *kilometres*).

- Keep calm if you can't answer each question immediately. If you can't answer a question, leave it out. Try to complete the missing answers during the second listening.

Unit check

1 Fill in the spaces

Complete the text with the words in the box.

> unafraid   unconcerned   through   which   who
> where   ghosts   across   ~~looking~~

I was ____looking____ through some old photos recently when I came [1] _____ one of Trevor,
[2] _____ was my favourite cousin. It reminded me of the summer I spent with him when I was eight.
He lived in a street [3] _____ had a lot of old, empty houses. At night, it was scary walking past
those houses, [4] _____ I thought I could hear noises and see faces at the windows. I imagined
[5] _____ going [6] _____ the walls. One night I awoke to see Trevor sitting on the window ledge
with his legs outside, talking. I called his name, but he was asleep. My aunt came in and took him back
to bed. She seemed [7] _____ about how close her son was to falling from the 2nd floor. "Oh, he's
always sleepwalked. He'll be fine." She was so calm and reassuring that I've been [8] _____ of
ghosts ever since.

| 9 |

2 Choose the correct answers

(Circle) the correct answer: a, b or c.

1 I love Italy, _____ you can get such great
   ice cream!
   a (where) b who c which

2 My sister works as _____ in Paris.
   a lawyer b a lawyer c the lawyer

3 Prague, _____ is the capital of the Czech Republic,
   is a great city.
   a where b who c which

4 This is the person _____ car was stolen.
   a that b who c whose

5 What's the name of the film _____ you saw?
   a that b where c who

6 Michael Jackson, _____ lived at Neverland,
   was a pop legend.
   a where b who c which

7 My parents always go to _____ early in the
   morning.
   a the work b a work c work

8 Genghis Khan, the great warrior, was afraid
   of _____ .
   a cats b a cat c the cats

9 It was difficult to _____ through such a
   boring film.
   a sit b go c sail

| 8 |

3 Vocabulary

Complete the sentences with a word beginning with a prefix.

1 It's really ____irresponsible____ to leave a dog in a hot car. Shame on you!
2 Isn't it _____ to go through a red light? Why didn't you stop?
3 There are some really _____ computers in the TechWorld sale – under £300.
4 They want people to wear _____ dress to their wedding. Strange, eh?
5 Pizza, burgers and crisps sounds like a very _____ diet to me.
6 It's very _____ to cough without covering your mouth.
7 I'm so tired! My new bed is so _____ that I couldn't get any sleep.
8 He's totally _____ about his test. He thinks he'll sail through it.
9 She's _____ to talk to you at the moment. She'll call you back.

| 8 |

How did you do?

Total: | 25 |

| 😊 | Very good
20 – 25 | 😐 | OK
14 – 19 | 😟 | Review Unit 13 again
0 – 13 |

14 Happiness

1 Grammar

✱ be used to

Match the two parts of the sentences. Then match the sentences with the pictures. Write 1–6 in the boxes.

1 I'm not used to getting up early,
2 We have to wear a uniform in our new school,
3 All the shops close at lunch time here
4 My little sister was sick,
5 My dad doesn't like his new office
6 Can I have a knife and fork please?

a and I don't like it because I'm used to wearing what I like.
b so I'm still really tired in the mornings.
c I'm not used to eating with chopsticks.
d because she's not used to travelling in the car.
e but I'm used to everything staying open all the time.
f because he's used to working from home.

 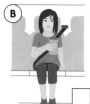    

A B C D [1] E F

2 Grammar

✱ used to doing vs. used to do

a Complete the sentences. Use the correct form of *used to* and the verbs in the box.

~~drive~~   eat   laugh   play   speak   wear

1 My father _used to drive_ a big, old, black Ford.
2 I _____ at his jokes, but now I think he's just stupid.
3 My mother _____ Spanish, but she's forgotten nearly all of it now.
4 _____ you _____ short trousers when you were a little boy?
5 My sister and I _____ video games together, but now she's left home.
6 I _____ (not) fast food, but now I eat it all the time!

b *be used to (doing)* or *used to (do)*? Complete the sentences with the correct form of the verbs.

1 When I was younger, I used to _speak_ (speak) French, but I've forgotten it all.

2 I'm used to _____ (get) lots of emails every day.

3 A: This coffee is very strong.
   B: No problem. I'm used to _____ (drink) strong coffee.

4 They didn't use to _____ (care) about what other people think of them.

5 He used to _____ (live) in a houseboat on the river Seine, but he had to sell the boat.

6 She used to _____ (run) for an hour every day, but she can't any more because of a problem with her knee.

7 Are you used to _____ (live) in Britain now, or do you still find it strange?

8 When he was young, he used to _____ (be) poor, but now he's rich and he's used to _____ (buy) anything he wants!

3 Vocabulary

★ Expressions with *feel*

a Paul wrote about his feelings in his computer diary. Read his diary entry and complete it. Circle the correct word: a, b, c or d.

About five years ago my favourite song was *'Baby I'm in love and I feel fine'* by the Beatles. It feels [1] ____strange____ to say that now that I <u>am</u> in love, I sometimes feel rather [2] _____ . For example, I feel a bit [3] _____ because I know that many other people are feeling [4] _____ while I'm in love. I really feel sorry for them. When I walk along the streets with my girlfriend, I also feel a bit [5] _____ . It seems all the world is looking at us! A week ago I felt [6] _____ to talk to my older brother about my problems. He says I should just feel [7] _____ that I will grow up. What does that mean? I am grown up. I'm just not feeling [8] _____ walking around holding hands with someone with other people staring at us! Oh, dear! I'm feeling [9] _____ – I'm so glad nobody can read this.

	a	b	c	d
1	up to	<u>strange</u>	cold	scared
2	sorry for	up to	the need	weird
3	up to	fine	guilty	comfortable
4	lonely	confident	fine	stupid
5	cold	up to	uncomfortable	fine
6	the need	cold	weird	lonely
7	the need	sorry for	confident	up to
8	comfortable	fine	up to	the need
9	the need	fine	cold	stupid

4 Grammar

✳ Phrasal verbs

a Complete the sentences with the correct form of one of the phrasal verbs in brackets.

1 We have a problem, but I'm sure we can ...*work*... it ...*out*.... . (work out / pick up)

2 I .... Nick the other day when I was in Oxford Street. (give up / bump into)

3 They didn't talk to each other for a year, but they have .... their problems .... now. (sort out / take after)

4 He really .... his mother's side of the family. (give up / take after)

5 We really cannot .... his behaviour any more! (put up / put up with)

6 We have to tell them the truth, we cannot just .... something .... (make up / give up)

7 This car is really old. I hope it's not going to .... (give up / break down)

8 Let's .... them .... Maybe they'll come along! (call up / make up)

b Put the words in the correct order to make sentences.

1 you / to / up / doesn't / look / he   *He doesn't look up to you.*

2 ran / he / from / away / her   ....

3 each / well / other / we / on / get / with   ....

4 our / forward / look / we / to / holidays   ....

5 put / for / night / a / can / we / up / him / with   ....

5 Pronunciation

✳ Stress in phrasal verbs

a ▶ CD3 T35 Listen and ⊙circle the prepositions that are weak. Underline the prepositions that are stressed.

1 a I think we can work it <u>out</u>.
  b He didn't say a word and ran (out) of the house.

2 a Pick your coat up.
  b She picked up her pen.

3 a I've given up sweets.
  b I've given them up.

4 a The plane took off.
  b He took off his shoes.

b ▶ CD3 T35 Listen again, check and repeat.

6 Vocabulary

Vocabulary bank Complete the sentences with the words in the box.

a~~ thing~~	the weather	at home	free
out of place	awful	feel	way

1 I'm just going to give you a small injection. You won't feel ......*a thing*...... .

2 The lights went out so we had to feel our .... to the emergency exit.

3 I feel .... about what I said to Danny about his girlfriend but someone had to tell him.

4 I felt really .... at the party so I left early.

5 I love visiting my Aunt Abi. She really makes me feel ....

6 I'm learning how to dance the tango and I'm just about getting the .... of it.

7 Feel .... to turn on the TV or use the computer while we're gone.

8 I don't think I'm going out tonight. I feel a bit under ....

7 Fiction in mind

a You are going to read an extract from 'A Matter of Chance'. Paul Morris's happy life in Italy changes when his wife dies suddenly. He develops an exciting relationship with Sandra, a friend at work. But all is not as it seems and Paul finds himself involved in a world of international crime.

While you read the extract, complete the text with the words in the box.

> been   alone   across   ~~had~~   to talk   all   that   life

Jacky. What can I tell you about Jacky?

I can tell you how she looked that bright February morning when she stepped out into the new sun, as the snow was falling off all the roofs, as she went out to buy something for a dress she was making. For a special dinner – we [1] _had_ been married for three years.

I have a film library of her in the back of my head: in the office; our first Christmas together, skiing in Scotland; the wedding; the trip [2] _____ France to our new home in Italy; and… and… I also have ten photographs of her that I took. Just ten out of the hundreds.

Afterwards, when I was able to, I looked through all the photos of our [3] _____ together and carefully chose the ten I liked best. I then had them enlarged, and put them in a special photo album. Which I have never opened since. [4] _____ this was many years ago. I am an old man now.

An old man full of memories, and full of thoughts about what could have [5] _____ .

An old man who often thinks about the way that one tiny chance happening can change someone's life: the roof-tile falls a second earlier or a second later, she goes towards a different shop, she goes towards the same shop a different way, she meets a friend and stops [6] _____ , she doesn't meet a friend and stop to talk, the traffic lights change as she gets to the crossing… or…

Such a tiny little chance [7] _____ she was there then and the roof-tile was there then. Such a tiny little chance that left me, at twenty-seven years of age, [8] _____ in a foreign country. Italy. So much hope. Such a bright future. Such an exciting thing to do. An adventure. To go and to start a new life in Italy.

(from Hill, D.A. (1999) 'A Matter of Chance', CUP: pp 7–9)

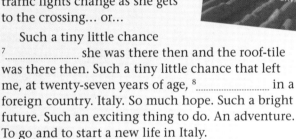

b Read the extract again and answer the questions.

1 What was the name of the narrator's wife? _____

2 Where was the narrator's wife killed? _____

3 How old was the narrator when his wife was killed? _____

4 Where did the tragic event happen? _____

8 Everyday English

b Underline the correct options.

1 A: I'm thirsty.
   B: Same *here / me*! Let's get a drink.

2 A: Do you like Thomas Groves?
   B: Yes I do! *Between / For* you and me, I'm hoping he'll ask me to go out one day.

3 I didn't want to apologise at first, but *on / in* the end, I thought it was the best thing to do.

4 No, I don't hate football. I just think there are better sports, *it's / that's* all.

5 A: London is the most beautiful city in the world.
   B: In *more / other* words you think it's more beautiful than Rome or Paris? You're mad!

6 A: Let's go into town.
   B: No, I'm really busy. Then *as well / again*, a break might be good for me. OK, let's go!

9 Write

a Read Joanne's composition about family life. Complete her text with the correct statements (a–f). There is one statement you won't need.

a However, it is also true that things are not always easy.

b On balance, how would I respond if I were asked if I wanted to leave home?

c Personally, I would not want to be on my own too soon.

d I would love to be totally independent.

e Many of my friends would love to be independent from their parents as soon as possible.

f It's great to be part of a happy family.

'Happiness is having a large, loving, caring family in another city.'
Discuss this statement and give your own opinion.

1 .... It is fun to be with people who like you. It is good to feel the warmth and the love of the ones who care for you. It is fantastic when you can turn to them when you have problems.

2 .... Young people want to develop their own personality. Parents often think they know better. They find it difficult to accept that their son or their daughter wants to live and think differently from how they used to live and think when they were young themselves. Consequently, young people are often frustrated and believe their parents do not understand them.

3 .... They would love to have their own place where they can live the life they imagine must be ideal. They think that not having a parent who tells them to tidy up their room or get up at a certain time must be paradise.

4 .... First of all, there is the financial situation. Having your own flat costs a lot of money. Secondly, being completely on your own also means a lot of responsibility. For example, I admit I like to be reminded occasionally of urgent things I have forgotten to do (although I would never admit that to my parents!). And thirdly, if members of a family accept that everybody is an individual and needs a certain amount of freedom, life in a family can be great fun.

5 .... I would say that I am happy living with my family for now and I'll wait.

---

b Write a composition of about 300 words to discuss the following statement and give your own opinion: 'The only way to happiness is by helping others.'

WRITING TIP

Developing a discursive composition (2)

- In order to make your points clearly and effectively, develop a clear progression of your argument.

- Decide how to introduce the topic, how to organise your ideas into paragraphs and how to conclude.

- Build each of your paragraphs around one particular point or idea. One effective way of doing this is to start each individual paragraph with a general statement (often called a topic sentence) to introduce the main idea of the paragraph. Add further sentences to support the idea.

Unit check

1 Fill in the spaces

Complete the text with the words in the box.

> told   used to   takes after   strange   ~~put me up~~
> puts up with   feel   look up to   sorry   felt

My cousin Anna ___put me up___ for a night when I visited London. Anna has five brothers and sisters, and her house is complete chaos. I'm ¹ _____ living with just my parents, so it felt ² _____ at first. I feel a bit ³ _____ for her – I really don't know how she ⁴ _____ all the noise! Her two younger sisters really ⁵ _____ her – they even copy the way she dresses and talks! Anna ⁶ _____ her mum, but when I mentioned this Anna ⁷ _____ me that everyone says this, so I ⁸ _____ a bit stupid. It wasn't very relaxing, but I enjoyed staying there, as they made me ⁹ _____ very welcome.

| 9 |

2 Choose the correct answers

Circle the correct answer: a, b or c.

1   When I was younger, I _____ speak Spanish.
    a (used to)   b was used to   c 'm used to

2   I'm used to _____ late.
    a stay up   b staying up   c stayed

3   I can't believe it. The car's broken _____ again.
    a up   b out   c down

4   He _____ into her at a party years later.
    a crashed   b bumped   c danced

5   I don't mind helping him. I'm used to _____ for others.
    a care   b caring   c caring about

6   I _____ to eat vegetables, but now I eat a lot.
    a didn't use   b didn't used   c used

7   He is cold because he is not used to _____ in a country like this.
    a live   b living   c lives

8   I shouldn't have done it. I'm really feeling _____!
    a up to   b fine   c guilty

9   After a year of living in Greece he'd _____ up the language perfectly.
    a picked   b talked   c taken

| 8 |

3 Vocabulary

Underline the correct words.

1   I'm feeling really *weird* / _confident_ / *lonely* about my driving test. I know I'm going to pass.

2   She's feeling a bit *beneath* / *below* / *under* the weather today. She's going to stay in bed.

3   Don't feel sorry *for* / *about* / *with* him. It's his own fault.

4   The dentist took out a tooth but I didn't feel a *pain* / *hurt* / *thing*.

5   It's hot. I'm on holiday. I feel the *want* / *need* / *wish* for an ice-cream!

6   It's normal to feel out of *room* / *place* / *face* on your first day at a new school.

7   I'd love to go on a long walk with you but I don't really feel *on* / *up* / *out* to it today.

8   Please feel *free* / *open* / *up* to take anything you want from the fridge.

9   I felt really *stupid* / *confident* / *strange* when I gave the teacher the wrong answer.

| 8 |

How did you do?

Total: | 25 |

|  Very good 20 – 25 | OK 14 – 19 |  Review Unit 14 again 0 – 13 |

Grammar reference

Unit 1

Past simple vs. present perfect simple

1 We use the past simple to talk about complete events which are finished, or before 'now', the moment of speaking.
   *I **called** you yesterday. Where **were** you?*
   *We **didn't have** computers when I **was** born.*

2 We use the present perfect simple to connect the past and 'now', the moment of speaking.
   *We've **called** you three times today. Where **have** you **been**?*
   *We've **lived** in the same house all our lives.*

3 Use the past simple with *minutes ago, yesterday, last week, when I was ...* etc.
   We often use *for, since, just, already, yet, ever* and *never* with the present perfect.

*They **went** out a few minutes **ago**.*	*They've **just left**.*
*I **saw** that film **yesterday**.*	*I've **already seen** that film.*
*I **met** her boyfriend **last weekend**.*	*I've **never met** your girlfriend.*
*We **moved** there **when I was young**.*	*We've **lived** there **since I was a child**.*

Time expressions

1 We use *just* before the past participle to say that something happened a short time ago.
   *We've **just arrived**.*   *They've **just gone** out.*

2 We use *already* at the end of the sentence or before the past participle to express surprise or emphasise that something happened.
   *Have you **finished already**?*   *We've **already seen** this film.*

3 We use *yet* at the end of negative sentences to emphasise that something didn't happen (but probably will in the future), and at the end of questions.
   *I **haven't started** this exercise **yet**. (but I will)*   *Have you **met** my new boyfriend **yet**?*

4 We use *still* before *haven't* in negative sentences, or before *not* in questions, to show surprise that something you expected to happen didn't happen.
   *I can't believe you **still haven't said** sorry.*   *Has she **still not told** you the truth?*

Unit 2

Past simple vs. past continuous

1 We use the past simple to talk about actions that happened at one moment in time in the past. We use the past continuous to describe the background actions in progress around that time in the past.

*I **was playing** football. (background)*	*I **broke** my leg. (action)*
*We **were having** a picnic. (background)*	*It **started** to rain. (action)*
*What **were** you **doing**? (background)*	*I **called** you. (action)*

2 It is common to use *when* with the past simple to introduce the past action, or *while* with the past continuous to introduce the background.
   *I **broke** my leg **while** I **was playing** football.*
   *We **were having** a picnic **when** it **started** to rain.*
   *What **were** you **doing when** I **called** you?*

Time conjunctions: *as / then / as soon as*

Other time words that we use with the past simple are *then* and *as soon as*. We can also use *as* with the same meaning as *while*.
***As soon as** I **got** home, I turned on the TV for the big game.*
*The picture came on, **then** I **learned** the bad news.*
*Someone scored **as** I **was making** a sandwich.*

Past simple vs. past perfect

1 We use the past simple to talk about an event that happened at a specific time in the past.
   We use the past perfect when we need to emphasise that one event happened <u>before</u> another.

*The match **had started** when we **got** there.*

*When I **got** to the street I **realised** I **hadn't brought** his address with me.*

*How long **had** you **been** there when they finally **arrived**?*

2 Sometimes it is necessary to use the past perfect to make the meaning clear.

*She'**d left** when I got there. (I didn't see her.)*

*She **left** when I got there. (but I saw her.)*

3 It is not necessary to use the past perfect when *before* or *after* is used.

*She left **before** I got there.*

Unit 3

Present perfect simple vs. present perfect continuous

1 We use the present perfect simple to emphasise the result or completion of an activity.

*I'**ve copied** that CD you asked me for. Here it is.*

*I'**ve bought** everybody's presents. Aren't I organised!*

We use the present perfect continuous to emphasise the activity, not the result or completion of the activity (it may not be finished).

*I'**ve been copying** CD's all morning. Great fun!*

*I'**ve been shopping** for presents. That's why I wasn't here.*

2 We use the present perfect simple to emphasise 'how many'.

*I'**ve done** ten exercises this morning.*　　　　*You'**ve had** three pieces of cake already!*

*How many sandwiches **have** you **made**?*

We use the present perfect continuous to emphasise 'how long'.

*I'**ve been doing** exercises for hours.*　　　　*You'**ve been eating** cake since you got here!*

*How long **have** you **been making** sandwiches?*

had better / should / ought to

We use *should* or *ought to* to give advice, or say what we think is a good (or bad) idea. They have the same meaning. Remember, *should* is a modal verb, and is used without *to*. We use *had better* to give stronger advice or warnings. The form is always past (never *have better*), but the meaning is present. *Had better* is also used without *to*.

*You **should** take a rest.*　　　　*You **shouldn't** worry so much.*

*She **ought to** be more careful.*　　　　*She **ought not to** be so pessimistic.*

*He'**d better** start doing some work.*　　　　*He'**d better not** come near me.*

Unit 4

Future predictions

100% probability	will	
↑	will probably	is likely
	might	might not
↓	probably won't	isn't likely to
0% probability	won't	

When we make predictions about the future, we can use *will*, *might* and *be likely to* (and their negative forms) to show how sure we are about the chances of something happening.

*My parents **will be** really angry when I get home tonight. (100% sure)*

*My father **will probably** / **is likely to shout** at me.*

*They **might not let** me **go out** again next weekend.*

*My brother **probably won't** / **isn't likely to help** me.*

*But next weekend, my parents **won't remember** what happened!*

First conditional with *if* and *unless*

In first conditional sentences:

a both verbs refer to actions or events in the future;

b the verb tense after the words *if* or *unless* is present simple;

c the verb tense in the other clause is *will* or *won't*;

d we can use *if* or *unless* (which means 'if not');

e   when we use *unless*, the verb that follows is in the positive.
*If my friends **visit** me (tomorrow), **we'll go** out for lunch.*
*I'll **take** them to the Chinese restaurant, unless they **want** to eat pizza. (= .... if they **don't want** to eat pizza.)*
*Unless my parents give me some money, I **won't be able** to pay. (= If my parents **don't give** …)*

Unit 5

make / let / be allowed to

1   We use *make [someone do]* to talk about an obligation.
*Our teacher **makes us do** a lot of homework. (= We cannot choose, it's an obligation that our teacher gives us.)*
*My older brother **made me lend** him some money. (= I could not choose, my brother forced me.)*

2   We use *let [someone do]* to talk about permission.
*Our teacher **lets us leave** early on Fridays. (= The teacher gives us permission to leave early.)*
*My father **let me use** the car yesterday. (= My father gave me permission to use the car.)*

3   We use *be allowed to [do something]* to say that someone has (or has not) got permission.
*At our school, we**'re allowed to wear** jeans if we want to.*
*When we were young, we **weren't allowed to play** outside in the street.*

Modals of obligation, prohibition and permission

1   *have to / don't have to* is used to talk about obligation / no obligation.
*We **don't have to wear** school uniform. (= Wearing school uniform is not an obligation for us.)*
*We **didn't have to pay** for the meal. (= It was not necessary to pay.)*

2   *can / can't* is used to talk about permission.
*You **can watch** TV if you want to. (= I give you permission to watch TV.)*
*We **can't go** in because we're not 18. (= We don't have permission to go in.)*

3   We use *mustn't* to prohibit someone from doing something, or to say that something is very important.
*We **mustn't be** late! (= It is very important for us not to be late.)*
*You **mustn't talk** to me like that! (= I am telling you that I don't allow this.)*

Unit 6

Present and past passive review

We form the passive with a form of the verb *to be* + the past participle of the main verb.
*English **is spoken** all over the world.*   *My bike **was stolen** last night.*

Causative *have* (*have something done*)

We use *have something done* when we talk about a service or function that someone else does for us.
*I **had my hair cut** last week. (= I went to a hairdresser and a person cut my hair.)*
*We've **had our car repaired**. (= We've taken our car to a garage and someone has repaired it for us.)*

Present perfect passive

We form the present perfect passive with *have/has been* + past participle.
*Our old house isn't there any more – it's **been pulled** down.*
*The rules of tennis **haven't been changed** for a long time.*

Future passive

We form the future passive with *will be / won't be* + past participle.
*Those trees **will be cut** down next month.*
*If you don't behave properly, you **won't be invited** again!*

Unit 7

Gerunds and infinitives

1   When a verb is followed by another verb, the second verb is either in the gerund (*-ing*) or infinitive form. The form of the second verb depends on the first verb.

2   Some verbs (e.g. *enjoy, detest, (don't) mind, imagine, feel like, suggest, practise, miss*) are followed by a verb in the gerund form.
*I don't **enjoy living** in the city very much.*   *She doesn't **feel like going** out tonight.*

3   Other verbs (e.g. *hope, promise, ask, learn, expect, decide, afford, offer, choose*) are followed by a verb in the infinitive form.
    *We can't **afford to go** on holiday this year.*   *I **promise to pay** you on Monday.*

Verbs with gerunds or infinitives

1   Some verbs (e.g. *remember, stop, try*) can be followed by a second verb in either the gerund or infinitive form. The form of the second verb depends on the meaning of the sentence.
    *I **remember going** to my first football match with my dad. (= I remember the occasion.)*
    *I **remembered to go** to the stadium and buy the tickets. (= I promised my son I would buy the tickets and I didn't forget to do this.)*
    *I **stopped to watch** the news headlines. (= I was doing something (my homework / talking to my parents) when the news started. I stopped the first activity because I wanted to watch the headlines.)*
    *I **stopped watching** TV and went to bed. (= I was watching TV. I was tired so I turned off the TV and went to bed.)*

2   Some verbs (e.g. *like, love, hate, prefer, begin, start*) can be followed by gerund or infinitive with no difference in meaning.
    *We **began to run** when it **started raining**.*   *We **began running** when it **started to rain**.*

Unit 8

Second conditional

1   When we want to talk about imaginary actions and their consequences, we use the second conditional.

2   The second conditional has two clauses; '*if* + the past tense' to introduce the hypothetical situation and '*would / could / might* + verb' to talk about the imaginary result.
    *If I **had** more time, I **would learn** the guitar.*

3   The clauses can be put the other way around. In this case we don't use a comma.
    *She **would be** the best student if she **worked** harder.*

4   Other ways of saying *if* in a second conditional include *what if, suppose, imagine* and *say*.
    ***What if** you won the lottery? Would you be happy?*
    ***Suppose** you could live forever. Would you want to?*
    ***Imagine** you knew your brother was a burglar. Would you tell the police?*
    ***Say** you could live anywhere. Where would you choose?*

I wish / if only

1   When we want to talk about how we would like our present life to be different, we can use *wish* or *if only* + past simple.

2   Although we are talking about our present situation, *wish / if only* are followed by the past tense.
    *I wish I **didn't have** so much homework.*   *Dave wishes he **had** a girlfriend.*

3   We use *wish / if only* + *could* when we want to talk about having the ability or permission to do something.
    *I wish I **could play** the guitar.*   *Sally wishes she **could go** to the party.*

Unit 9

Linkers of contrast: *however / although / even though / in spite of / despite*

1   *Despite* and *in spite of* are followed by a noun or verb in the gerund form.
    ***Despite** being very rich, he's not happy.*   ***In spite of** his wealth, he's not very happy.*

2   *Although* and *even though* are followed by a clause.
    ***Although** they played badly, they still won.*
    ***Even though** he's lived in Paris for three years, he doesn't speak French.*

3   *However* always starts a new sentence.
    *I don't usually like action films. **However**, I really enjoyed Troy.*

Modals of deduction (present)

1   When we are sure something is true, we use *must*.
    *She got ten Valentine cards. She **must** be popular.*

2   When we are sure something is not true, we use *can't*.
    *He's failed the driving test five times. He **can't** be a very good driver.*

3   When we think there is a possibility something is true, we use *might* or *could*.
    *They're speaking Spanish so they **might** be Mexican.*
    *They **could** be brother and sister. They look quite similar.*

Unit 10

Modals of deduction (past)

To make a guess about a past situation, we can use the modal verbs *can't*, *must*, *might* and *could* with the present perfect tense.
*You were all alone in the house. You **must have been** really scared.*
*I'm not sure how the vase got broken but it **might have been** the dog.*
*Police believe that the criminal **could have left** the country.*
*It **can't have been** my husband. He was at home with me all last night.*

Indirect questions

1   After expressions like *I don't understand …, I wonder …, I want to know …* and *I don't know …* we often find question words. However, what comes after the question word is not a question, and does not follow the word order for questions.
    *I wonder **why she said that**. (**NOT** I wonder why ~~did she say that~~.)*
    *I don't know **when we'll arrive**. (**NOT** I don't know when ~~will we arrive~~.)*
    *I want to know **where you're going**. (**NOT** I want to know where ~~are you going~~.)*

2   If we want to ask less direct questions, we can use an expression such as *Can you tell me …, Do you happen to know …* and *Do you know … .* This is the question, so what comes after these expressions does not follow the word order for questions.
    *Can you tell me **where the toilets are**? (**NOT** Can you tell me where ~~are the toilets~~?)*
    *Do you happen to know **if he's French**? (**NOT** Do you happen to know ~~is he French~~?)*
    *Do you know **why she left early**? (**NOT** Do you know why ~~did she leave early~~?)*

Unit 11

Reported statements (review)

In reported speech, we often change the verb that was used in direct speech.

'It's late,' he said.	→	*He said it **was** late.*
'I've lost my watch,' she said.	→	*She said she**'d lost** her watch.*
*'We **didn't enjoy** our holiday,' they said.*	→	*They said they **hadn't enjoyed** their holiday.*
*'I **can't open** the door,' my sister said.*	→	*My sister said she **couldn't open** the door.*
*'I**'ll pick** you up at eight,' she said.*	→	*She said she**'d pick** me up at eight.*

Reported questions

1   When we report yes/no questions, we use *if* (or *whether*) and statement word order.

'Is London very big?'	→	*He asked me **if** London was big.*
'Do you play chess?'	→	*She asked me **whether** I played chess.*
'Did your father go abroad last year?'	→	*He asked me **if** my father had gone abroad last year.*

2   When we report *wh-* questions (with *who / where / what / how / when* etc.), we use the same question word and statement word order.

'Who are you talking to?'	→	*He asked me **who** I was talking to.*
'When did you arrive?'	→	*They asked me **when** I had arrived.*
'How much money have you got?'	→	*She asked me **how much** money I'd got.*

3   With requests, we use *'asked'* + person + *to (do)*.

'Please carry this for me, Mike.'	→	*She **asked Mike to carry** it for her.*
'Can you open the window please?'	→	*He **asked me to open** the window.*
'Please don't be late!'	→	*The teacher **asked us not to be** late.*

Reporting verbs

We can use many different verbs to report speech. Be careful about the pattern that follows these verbs.

1   Some verbs (e.g. *say, explain*) are followed by *that* + clause.
    *He **said that** the film was one of the best he'd ever seen.*
    *She **explained that** she couldn't come because she had work to do.*

2   Some verbs (e.g. *offer, refuse, agree*) are followed by the infinitive with *to*.
    *My mother **offered to lend** me some money.*
    *She **refused to tell** me her name.*
    *I **agreed to go** with them.*

3   Some verbs (e.g. *ask, order, invite, tell, persuade*) are followed by an object + infinitive with *to*.
    *My father **asked my sister to help** him choose a present for my mother.*
    *The policeman **ordered them to stop**.*
    *My grandparents **invited me to have** lunch with them.*
    *Our teacher **told us to concentrate** more.*
    *My friends **persuaded me to go** to the concert with them.*

4   Some verbs (e.g. *apologise for, suggest*) are followed by a noun or a gerund.
    *He **apologised for the noise / making** a noise.*
    *She **suggested a walk / going** for a walk.*

Unit 12

Third conditional

1   We use the third conditional to speculate about how things might have been different in the past.
    The third conditional is formed with *If* + past perfect + *would (not) have* + past participle.
    *If we'd **waited** for you, we **would have missed** the beginning of the film.*
    (= We <u>didn't</u> wait for you, so we <u>didn't</u> miss the beginning of the film.)
    *If you **hadn't fallen asleep** in the lesson, the teacher **wouldn't have made** you stay after school.*
    (= You <u>did</u> fall asleep and the teacher <u>did</u> make you stay after school.)

2   Instead of *would*, we can use *might* (if we are not very sure of the possible result).
    *If we'd **waited** for you, we **might have missed** the beginning of the film.*

I wish / If only + for past situations

We use *I wish* or *If only* + past perfect to express regret about past actions or events.
*I wish I'd **phoned** her.* (= I <u>didn't</u> phone her, and I regret it.)
*I wish they **hadn't told** you about it.* (= They <u>did</u> tell you, and I regret it.)
*If only I'd **studied** harder.* (= I <u>didn't</u> study hard, and I regret it.)
*If only we **hadn't argued** with them.* (= We <u>did</u> argue with them, and I regret it.)

should have done

We use *should / shouldn't have (done)* to criticise past actions.
*You **should've told** me.* (= You <u>didn't</u> tell me, and I think that was wrong.)
*She **shouldn't have broken** my camera.* (= She <u>did</u> break my camera, and that was wrong.)

Unit 13

Defining and non-defining relative clauses

1   We use relative clauses to add information about the subject or object of a sentence.

2   Relative clauses are introduced by words like *that, which, where, who* and *whose*.

    We use *that / which* to refer to things.
    *That's the car **that / which** almost killed me.*

    We use *that / who* to refer to people.
    *The woman **who / that** served me was American.*

    We use *where* to refer to places.
    *These photos were taken in Paris, **where** we went for our holiday last year.*

    We use *whose* to refer to possession.
    *She's the girl **whose** brother plays football for Liverpool.*

3   Sometimes the information is essential to know what exactly we are talking about. In these cases we use
    a defining relative clause and we don't use a comma.
    *My brother **who** lives in Canada is an architect.*
    (= I have more than one brother but I am talking about the one who lives in Canada.)

4 Sometimes the information is additional. We don't need it to understand what we are talking about. This is a non-defining relative clause. The extra information is included between commas. (NB In these sentences we <u>can't</u> use *that*.) For example:

*My brother, **who lives in Canada**, is an architect.*

(= I only have one brother. He lives in Canada and is an architect.)

Definite, indefinite and zero article

1 We use the definite article (*the*):

a when something is unique: Have you seen ***the*** moon tonight? It's beautiful.

b to talk about the ability to play an instrument: She's plays ***the*** violin really well.

c to refer to specific things: I love ***the*** sound of birds singing in the morning.

d when we know what is being talked about: Have you got ***the*** money? (= I lent you last week.)

2 We use the indefinite article (*a/an*):

a to talk about professions: My dad's ***a*** teacher.

b to talk about <u>a</u> not one thing: I read ***a*** really good book last week.

3 We use the zero article (no article):

a to refer to things in general: ***Music*** always makes me feel happy.

b to talk about places as institutions: I go to ***church*** about twice a month.

Unit 14

be used to doing vs. *used to do*

1 When we want to say that we are accustomed or not to doing things, we can use the expressions *be used to* and *get used to*. These expressions are followed by a noun or the gerund (*-ing*) form of a verb.

*He's not used to **being** so popular.*   *She's not really used to young **children**.*

2 *be used to* refers to a state.

*I'm not **used to working** so hard.*

3 *get used to* refers to the process.

*It took me years **to get used to driving** on the left.*

4 Don't confuse these expressions with *used to*, which refers to past habits and is followed by an infinitive without *to*.

*We **used to spend** our holidays in the south of France when I was a child.*

Phrasal verbs

1 Phrasal verbs have two or three parts.

*Guess who I **bumped into** yesterday? (met by chance)*

*I really **look up to** my Maths teacher. (respect)*

2 With some phrasal verbs, these parts can be separated by the object of the verb.

*I **called up** my friend as soon as I heard the news.* OR

*I **called** my friend **up** as soon as I heard the news.*

However, when the object is a pronoun, it must come between the two parts.

*I called **him** up. (**NOT** ~~I called up him.~~)*

3 In other phrasal verbs, these parts can never be separated.

*I **take after** my mother. (**NOT** ~~I take my mother after.~~)*

4 Three part phrasal verbs cannot be split.

*I've **made up with** my girlfriend.*

5 To find out if a phrasal verb can be split or not, look in a dictionary:

If it **can** be split, it will be listed: *call <u>sb</u> up*

If it **can't** be split, it will be listed: *take after <u>sb</u>*

6 Some phrasal verbs have more than one meaning.

*My car's **broken down**. (stopped working)*

*When she heard the news, she **broke down**. (started crying)*